MORE
HOLINESS
GIVE ME

MORE HOLINESS GIVE ME

ROBERT L. MILLET

DESERET
BOOK

Library of Congress Cataloging-in-Publication Data

Millet, Robert L.
  More holiness give me / Robert L. Millet.
    p. cm.
  Includes bibliographical references and index.
  ISBN 1-57345-920-8 (hardbound : alk. paper)
    1. Christian life—Mormon authors. 2. Church of Jesus Christ of Latter-day Saints—Doctrines. 3. Mormon Church—Doctrines. I. Title.

  BX8656 .M544 2001
  248.4'89332—dc21   2001000293

Printed in the United States of America   72082-6792

10 9 8 7 6 5 4 3 2 1

CONTENTS

PREFACE

THE SON OF MAN OF HOLINESS spoke to the ancient law-giver on Mount Horeb: "Draw not nigh hither: put off thy shoes from off thy feet, for the place whereon thou standest is holy ground" (Exodus 3:5). Later that same divine being spoke through Moses to the nation of Israel: "Now therefore, if ye will obey my voice indeed, and keep my covenant, then ye shall be a peculiar treasure unto me above all people: for all the earth is mine: and ye shall be unto me a kingdom of priests, and an holy nation" (Exodus 19:5–6).

A millennium and a half later the apostle Peter reminded the Saints scattered abroad that "as he which hath called you is holy, so be ye holy in all manner of conversation [conduct]; because it is written, Be ye holy; for I am holy" (1 Peter 1:15–16; see also Leviticus 11:44).

Indeed, in all ages of time, whenever the gospel of Jesus Christ has been on the earth, the God of heaven (who is Holy) has called and commissioned his children to "be a special people unto himself, above all people that are upon the face of the earth" (Deuteronomy 7:6). To do this, it has always been necessary for those who aspired to holiness to "put [a] difference

between holy and unholy, and between unclean and clean"
(Leviticus 10:10), to draw the line between righteousness and
unrighteousness. This is a book about holiness, about becoming separate and apart from the world while remaining in the
world. I am persuaded that this is a study worthy of our time,
an investigation that results in profound insights, for "the fear
of the Lord is the beginning of wisdom: and the knowledge of
the holy is understanding" (Proverbs 9:10).

The pages that follow contain no lists of things to do, no
formulas for achieving holiness. Rather, they reflect briefly but
soberly upon some matters that the scriptures and the
prophets, ancient and modern, have associated with becoming
a holy person. Holiness may be said to begin with being born
again, which is a multifaceted spiritual process, for our God,
who is all-wise and all-powerful, is hardly confined to one
avenue of change when it comes to purifying and renewing his
children. Consequently we speak of being reborn in terms of
being crucified with Christ, having our souls healed, moving
from darkness to light, becoming as a little child, being baptized by fire, gaining the mind of Christ, speaking with the
tongue of angels, and being spiritually liberated.

Likewise, becoming holy—a lifetime pursuit, to be sure—
touches upon many phases of our life, and growing in holiness
is manifest in diverse and varied ways: being washed in the
blood of the Lamb, choosing to climb to new spiritual heights,
making every day holy, making decisions with eternal consequence, gaining victory over self and becoming conscious of
the same, facing difficulties with greater maturity, becoming
more stable and secure in the faith, delighting more regularly
in the wonders of God and his creations, and viewing and
treating others as the Almighty does.

As with any published work, I am indebted to many people who over the years have advised me, counseled me, and encouraged me to exercise a lively hope in Christ—to believe that God loves us all and is willing and eager, through the mediation of his Beloved Son, to save as many of us as will be saved. In the preparation of this book I especially appreciate the work of Lori Soza, a conscientious assistant and trusted colleague. And Suzanne Brady of Deseret Book Company has again struck that delicate balance as an editor: she has allowed me to maintain my own style of writing while at the same time tightening the organization and sharpening the clarity of expression. I count Suzanne not only as a capable professional but also as a valued friend.

Nonetheless, I alone am responsible for the conclusions drawn from the evidence cited. This book is a private endeavor and not an official publication of either The Church of Jesus Christ of Latter-day Saints or of Brigham Young University. I write of the things contained herein not from a position of one who is holy but rather as one who seeks understanding on this significant topic and, more important, as one who longs to become holy. For me, as with most of humankind, the ideal is yet to become an unblemished reality. But we have a sure and certain hope in Christ.

As Amulek explained to the Zoramites, "this life is the time for men to prepare to meet God" (Alma 34:32). Now is the time for us to prepare ourselves for what lies ahead. My soul resonates with this bold invitation to holiness from the Prophet Joseph Smith:

"When I contemplate the rapidity with which the great and glorious day of the coming of the Son of Man advances, when He shall come to receive His Saints unto Himself, where they shall dwell in His presence, and be crowned with glory and immortality . . . I cry out in my heart, What manner of persons ought we to be in all holy conversation and godliness!" (*Teachings of the Prophet Joseph Smith,* 29; see also 1 Peter 3:10–11).

Is This All There Is?

Y EARS AGO WHILE SERVING AS a bishop, I would sit on the stand during sacrament meeting and look out over the congregation. Each time there welled up within me a deep love and profound appreciation for the goodness and commitment of the Latter-day Saints. These were men and women of faith, persons who had given themselves fully to the cause of the restored gospel. On one particular day, my eyes fastened on a young couple (let's call them the Barretts) near the back of the chapel. They had been in the ward for a few years and had served faithfully, he in the elders quorum and she in the Relief Society. They had four little boys, active but handsome and bright. I sensed that the husband and wife needed to speak with me, but I quickly dismissed the impression, knowing how well they seemed to be doing and also knowing of others in the ward—not doing so well—who needed my more immediate attention that day.

The same thought occurred to me several times over the next few months (I'm sometimes a bit slow in receiving guidance!), until finally I asked my executive secretary to invite the man and his wife in to see me during the following week. We chatted cordially for about fifteen minutes, and I finally got around to asking a question that I have found as a priesthood leader to be quite helpful: "You two have been on my mind for a while. Why do you suppose I have been thinking about you so much?" The husband made a humorous comment, but the wife responded more seriously: "Bishop, we really are glad that you asked us to visit with you. There are some things we've been discussing as a couple for about a year now that we felt we should mention to you." I should add quickly that all was well in terms of their worthiness and their "activity"—that is, they attended all their meetings, performed their Church assignments regularly, and held a current temple recommend. But all was not well in terms of their spirituality.

Brother Barrett continued: "Bishop, Cindy and I have been active members of the Church all our lives. We both had wonderful parents, who brought us to Church and involved us in all the things that LDS families do. I served an honorable mission, we were married worthily in the temple, and we now have four beautiful children. I work at a job that I enjoy, and we are blessed with an income that allows us many luxuries. Supposedly we have everything a couple could ask for, but our questions are, Is this it? Is this all there is? Is this what we prepared all our lives for? Where do we go from here?"

We had a lengthy chat that evening—and a few visits subsequently—to discuss what happiness is, what spirituality is all about, what the Church can and cannot do for us, and what lay ahead. The conversations were warm and friendly; their comments and questions, genuine and candid. There was no doubt and cynicism in their approach, only searching queries about expectations and realities.

I watched this couple with much interest over the next several years and have been pleased to witness their progress and what seems to be a resolution of some of their more vexing concerns. Yet the memory of our conversations haunts me. I have come to realize that their concerns were in no way unusual or out of the ordinary. In fact, they were simply being more honest than I had been at their age, more eager to get at the root of dilemmas than I had been. I realize now that their questions are in fact hidden deep within the hearts of many Latter-day Saints and that each of us, at one time or another, wrestles with what life is all about and what it takes to be content. It is sobering to know that someone can possess the fulness of the gospel, have the insights and perspective that come through membership in the Lord's Church and kingdom, be fully engaged in the work of the Church, and still feel empty and unsatisfied.

There really is a difference between having a genuine, Spirit-given witness of this work and being fully converted to the Lord and his work. Acquiring a testimony of the gospel of Jesus Christ is a remarkable thing. It is a miracle, an instance in which the Infinite impacts the finite, in which the heavens touch the earth, in which Spirit speaks to spirit, in which God manifests truth to mortals. To gain a testimony is to be reborn as to what we know and feel and value. One who has received such a manifestation is a new creature, a new creature in Christ.

By the power of the Spirit we come to know the things of God: we gain a testimony. By that same power we continue the process of *conversion*. In a sense, gaining a testimony is a form of conversion from unbelief to belief, from doubt to certitude. The process of conversion—the process by which we are changed from a carnal and fallen state to a state of righteousness (Mosiah 27:25)—continues throughout our lives. Conversion "denotes changing one's views, in a conscious acceptance of the will of God (Acts 3:19). If followed by continued faith in the Lord Jesus Christ, repentance, baptism in water for the remission of sins, and the reception of the Holy Ghost by the laying on of hands, conversion will become complete, and will change a natural man into a sanctified, born again, purified person—a new creature in Christ Jesus (see 2 Cor. 5:17)."[1] "To become converted, according to the scriptures, means having a change of heart and the moral character of a person turned from the controlled power of sin into a righteous life. . . . It means to overcome the tendencies to criticize and to strive continually to improve inward weaknesses and not merely the outward appearances."[2]

Since the time I met with the Barretts, it has become clear to me that many of us confuse means with ends, and in the process of doing so we trip over priorities and lose track of things that matter most. Tom Barrett had been brought up to believe that a full-time mission was, in a sense, a great end. Both Cindy and Tom had come to believe that a temple marriage was likewise a great end, something we work to achieve in spite of all odds. To be sure, missions and marriage are significant events in one's eternal journey, for they lay a foundation for life here and hereafter. But they are only a moment, a foundation upon which we must build our houses of faith. They are not ends in themselves but rather means to a greater end. When members of the Church view them as ends, it is not surprising that they eventually ask aloud (or in their hearts) about their lives to that point, "Is this all there is?"

Even matters that should receive the greatest focus in the Church—covenants, ordinances, sealings, and so forth—are means to an end. They have been given to us by a gracious God to empower us to "come unto Christ and be perfected in him" (Moroni 10:32; D&C 20:59). We go to Church, serve others, search the scriptures, fast and pray, participate in the ordinances of the temple in an effort to bridge the chasm between us and the heavens, to gain fellowship with our Heavenly Father and his Son Jesus Christ (1 John 1:3).

We teach and we listen, we minister and we receive counsel, we serve long hours in our assignments, all to the end that we might grow up in the Lord and eventually receive a fulness of the Holy Ghost (D&C 109:15). The Prophet Joseph Smith declared that "happiness is the object and design of our existence; and will be the end thereof, if we pursue the path that leads to it; and this path is virtue, uprightness, faithfulness, holiness, and keeping all the commandments of God."[3] It is a long path, a strait path, a mountainous path that winds and curls and ascends, a journey that requires faith and energy and perseverance to reach the top. There are intermediate stops along the way, summits and plateaus that provide temporary rest and reassurance. But climbers will not find ultimate satisfaction unless they are pressing toward the top of the mountain. And so it is with life.

The Savior taught, "In the world ye shall have tribulation: but be of good cheer; I have overcome the world" (John 16:33). In a modern revelation that same Lord declared, "Wherefore, fear not even unto death; for in this world your joy is not full, but in me your joy is full" (D&C 101:36). Our joy is to be found in and through Christ. Our ultimate satisfaction with family, friends, occupation will come only as the light of the Lord shines upon those relationships endeavors, only as his healing hand is placed upon them. Any activity, though noble of itself, will, as a means to a greater end, always come short of what could be enjoyed through engagement with him who is the Great End. To climb the mountain of spirituality is to "press toward the mark for the prize of the high calling of God in Christ Jesus" (Philippians 3:14).

NOTES

1. LDS Bible Dictionary, s.v. "conversion."
2. Lee, *Stand Ye in Holy Places,* 354–55.
3. *Teachings of the Prophet Joseph Smith,* 255–56.

CHAPTER 1

WHERE ART THOU?

IN THAT FASCINATING STORY IN the opening chapters of the Bible, Adam and Eve have partaken of the forbidden fruit, hidden themselves from God, and now hear the divine inquiry: "Where art thou?" (Genesis 3:9). Philosophers and theologians have for centuries found much to discuss and debate about this episode: Why would an all-knowing God ask such a question? Did God not know where our first parents were? Dennis Rasmussen has insightfully written: "When Adam left Eden, the Lord clothed his body with a garment and his soul with a question. Adam, where art thou? Does God not know? On the contrary, only he knows. In my weakness I lose my bearings. Like a child wandering in a forest I follow the whims of the moment and forget the way. I am too caught up by my surroundings to follow the path. Not until a Father's voice calls do I wonder where I am. How shall I answer? I am here? But where is here? So helpless am I that I cannot say. But deep within I hear his voice and tremble, for finally there are just two places, with him or without him, and just two ways, toward him or not toward him."[1]

We need to know where we are if we are to move forward, for forward and backward are relatively meaningless concepts or directions until we discover our present location. We might well ask with the psalmist, "What is man, that thou art mindful of him?" (Psalm 8:4). Is man, as most of the Christian world proclaims, a depraved creature, an animal bent on evil and carnality? Or, as some affirm, is man a noble and God-fearing creation, a being prone to do good and contribute with purpose and meaning? On the one hand, we can certainly see the value of focusing on the goodness of man, for such an approach seems much more invigorating and uplifting. On the other hand, the scriptures surely speak of this mortal sphere as a telestial existence, a state in which all forms of life are lost and fallen. What shall we believe? Adam, where art thou? Eve, where art thou?

The scriptures of the Restoration open the gates for a marvelous flood of light concerning the nature of man, his origin, and his destiny. The Lord revealed through Joseph Smith that man is an eternal being. The Prophet Joseph declared that the intelligence of man "is not a created being; it existed from eternity, and will exist to eternity. Anything created cannot be eternal."[2] In his marvelous King Follett Discourse, delivered less than three months before his martyrdom, the Prophet said: "We say that God himself is a self-existent being. Who told you so? It is correct enough; but how did it get into your heads? Who told you that man did not exist in like manner upon the same principles? Man does exist upon the same principles. . . . The mind or the intelligence which man possesses is co-equal [meaning, co-eternal or coeval] with God himself. . . . The intelligence of spirits had no beginning, neither will it have an end. There never was a time when there were not spirits. . . . I take my ring from my finger and liken it unto the mind of man—the immortal part, because it has no beginning. Suppose you cut it in two; then it has a beginning and an end; but join it again, and it continues one eternal round. So with the spirit of man."[3]

More specifically, the revelations set forth the profound truth that men and women "were also in the beginning with the Father; that which is Spirit, even the Spirit of truth" (D&C 93:23). During the administration of President Joseph F. Smith, an official pronouncement by the First Presidency stated that "all men and women are in the similitude of the universal Father and Mother, and are literally the sons and daughters of Deity." Further, "the doctrine of the pre-existence—revealed so plainly, particularly in latter days, pours a wonderful flood of light upon the otherwise mysterious problem of man's origin. It shows that man, as a spirit, was begotten and born of heavenly parents, and reared to maturity in the eternal mansions of the father, prior to coming upon the earth in a temporal body to undergo an experience in mortality. It teaches that all men existed in the spirit before any man existed in the flesh, and that all who have inhabited the earth since Adam have taken bodies and become souls in like manner."[4]

As gods in embryo, we have received the attributes, powers, and capacities possessed by our Father in Heaven; they have been transmitted to us; they are a part of us. "We believe that we are the offspring of our Father in heaven," President Lorenzo Snow observed, "and that we possess in our spiritual organizations the same capabilities, powers and faculties that our Father possesses, although in an infantile state, requiring to pass through a certain course or ordeal by which they will be developed and improved according to the heed we give to the principles we have received."[5] Thus there is a sense in which we might say that men and women, being spiritual heirs to godhood, are good by nature; that is, they are good because they are related to and products of the Highest Good. God is good, even the embodiment and personification of all that is noble, upright, and edifying, and we are from him.

In consequence of the belief in human depravity held by many in the nineteenth century, the doctrines of the Restoration were a refreshing breeze in a dry and arid spiritual climate. The revealed word that God had forgiven Adam's transgression and the corollary principle that little children who die before the age of accountability are saved—these beliefs set the Latter-day Saints apart from much of the Christian world and certainly painted a more optimistic picture in regard to the nature of man. And yet the spirit, the eternal part of us, can be and is influenced by our fallen nature, our flesh. "Now I want to tell you," President Brigham Young pointed out, "that [Satan] does not hold any power over man, only so far as the body overcomes the spirit that is in a man, through yielding to the spirit of evil. The spirit that the Lord puts into a tabernacle of flesh is under the dictation of the Lord Almighty; but the spirit and body are united in order that the spirit may have a tabernacle, and be exalted; and the spirit is influenced by the body, and the body by the spirit. In the first place the spirit is pure, and under the special control and influence of the Lord, but the body is . . . under the mighty influence of that fallen nature that is of the earth."[6] Hence the debate between those who argue for man's nobility and those who argue for man's ignobility is resolved by asking, With which nature do we concern ourselves? Man is basically good—at least, his eternal nature is. Man is basically fallen—at least, his mortal nature is.

We know that because Adam and Eve transgressed by partaking of the forbidden fruit, they were cast from the Garden of Eden and from the presence of the Lord, which is spiritual death. As a result came blood, sweat, toil, opposition, bodily decay, and, finally, physical death. Even though the Fall was a vital part of the great plan of the Eternal God—as much a foreordained act as Christ's intercession—our state, including our relationship with God, changed dramatically. Early in the Nephite record, Lehi "spake concerning the prophets, how great a number had testified of . . . [the] Redeemer of the world. Wherefore, all mankind were in a lost and in a fallen state, and ever would be save they should rely on this Redeemer" (1 Nephi 10:5–6). Joseph Smith wrote to John Wentworth: "We believe that men will be punished for their own sins, and not for Adam's transgression" (Articles of Faith 1:2). The Lord affirms that principle in his statement to Adam: "I have forgiven thee thy transgression in the Garden of Eden" (Moses 6:53). This declaration must, however, be understood in the proper doctrinal context. Although God forgave our first parents their transgression, although no "original sin" is entailed upon the children of Adam and Eve, and although "the Son of God hath atoned for original guilt, wherein the sins of the parents cannot be answered upon the heads of the children" (Moses 6:54), we must not minimize the effects of the Fall.

To say that we are not condemned by the fall of Adam is not to say that we are unaffected by it. Jehovah explained to Adam: "Inasmuch as thy children are *conceived in sin,* even so when they begin to grow up, sin conceiveth in their hearts, and they taste the bitter, that they may know to prize the good" (Moses 6:55; italics added). Joseph Smith did not believe, with Calvin, in the moral depravity of humanity. He did not believe, with Luther, that human beings, because of intrinsic carnality and depravity, do not even have the power to choose good over evil. He did not believe that children are born in sin, that they inherit the so-called sin of Adam, either through the sexual union or by birth. Rather, children are conceived in sin, meaning, first, that they are conceived into a world of sin, and second, that conception is the vehicle by which the effects of the Fall (not the original guilt, which God has forgiven) are transmitted to Adam and Eve's posterity. There is no sin in sexual union within the bonds of marriage, nor is conception itself sinful. Rather, through conception the fallen nature—mortality, or what the scriptures call the flesh—originates; through the process of becoming mortal, one inherits the effects of the fall of Adam, both physical and spiritual.

To say that men and women are not punished for the transgression of Adam is not to say that we are not subject to it or affected by it. In fact, Lehi taught Jacob that in the beginning God "gave commandment that all men must repent; for he showed unto all men that they were lost, because of the transgression of their parents" (2 Nephi 2:21; compare Alma 22:14). Thus we all need to repent, because we all have the ability, the propensity, to sin, because we inherited Adam and Eve's fallen nature. "We know that thou art holy," the brother of Jared confessed to the Almighty, "and dwellest in the heavens, and that we are unworthy before thee; *because of the fall our natures have become evil continually;* nevertheless, O Lord, thou hast given us a commandment that we must call upon thee, that from thee we may receive according to our desires" (Ether 3:2; italics added).

Conception, which clothes us in the flesh, is the mechanism of transmission, the means by which Adam and Eve's fallen nature (both physical and spiritual death) is transferred from generation to generation. The propensity for sin and our susceptibility to it are implanted in our nature at conception, just as death is. Both death and sin are present only as potentialities at conception, and therefore neither is fully evident at birth. Death and sin do, however, become actual parts of our nature as we grow up. Sin comes spontaneously, just as death does. In the case of little children, responsibility for the results of this fallen nature (sinful actions and dispositions) are held in abeyance by virtue of the Atonement until they reach the age of accountability. When children reach the time of accountability, however, they become subject to spiritual death and must thereafter repent and come unto Christ by covenant and through the ordinances of the gospel. "I have learned in my travels," the Prophet Joseph Smith observed, "that man is treacherous and selfish, but few excepted."[7] "Men have been ever prone to apostasy," Elder John Taylor pointed out. "Our fallen nature is at enmity with a godly life."[8]

In setting forth the doctrine of atonement, King Benjamin taught: "The natural man is an enemy to God, and has been from the fall of Adam, and will be, forever and ever, unless he yields to the enticings of the Holy Spirit, and putteth off the natural man and becometh a saint through the atonement of Christ the Lord" (Mosiah 3:19). What is King Benjamin saying about humanity? What is the natural man, and how may he be characterized? Natural men and women are unregenerated beings who remain in their fallen condition, living without God and godliness in the world. They are unredeemed creatures without comfort, beings who live by their own light. On the one hand, natural men and women may be people bent on lechery and lasciviousness; they may love Satan more than God and therefore be "carnal, sensual, and devilish" (Moses 5:13). After having preached to and pleaded with his son Corianton and after having taught him that "wickedness never was happiness," Alma said, "And now, my son, all men that are in a state of nature, or I would say, in a carnal state, are in the gall of bitterness and in the bonds of iniquity." Now note how such persons are enemies to God: "They are without God in the world, and they have gone contrary to the nature of God; therefore, they are in a state contrary to the nature of happiness" (Alma 41:10–11).

Natural men and women need not, however, be what we would call degenerate. They may well be moral and upright men and women, bent upon goodness and benevolence. Nevertheless, they are acclimated to the present fallen world. Such persons do not enjoy the enlivening powers of the Holy Ghost: they have not received the revealed witness of the truth, and they have not enjoyed the sanctifying powers of the blood of Christ. Although their behavior is proper and appropriate according to societal standards, these natural men and women have not hearkened sufficiently to the Light of Christ to be led to the covenant gospel (Mosiah 16:2; see also D&C 84:45–48). "The whole world lieth in sin," the Savior declared in a modern revelation, "and groaneth under darkness and under the bondage of sin. And by this you may know they are under the bondage of sin, because they come not unto me" (D&C 84:49–50; see also 35:12).

And what of the members of The Church of Jesus Christ of

Latter-day Saints? "There is no doubt," President Brigham Young stated, "if a person lives according to the revelations given to God's people, he may have the Spirit of the Lord to signify to him His will, and to guide and to direct him in the discharge of his duties, in his temporal as well as his spiritual exercises. I am satisfied, however, that in this respect, we live far beneath our privileges."⁹ Members of the Church who refuse to climb toward greater spiritual heights, who have no inclination to further anchor themselves in the truth, who have become satisfied with their present spiritual state—these are they who are natural men and women, persons generally of good will who do not understand that through their smugness and complacency they are aiding and abetting the cause of the enemy of all righteousness.

Because of the Fall, all men and women are lost, fallen, and alienated from God and things of righteousness; they suffer spiritual death (Alma 12:16; 40:26; 42:9; D&C 29:41). That is the harsh reality of our second estate. The glad tidings, the good news, is that redemption from the Fall and reconciliation with the Father are possible. That redemption and reconciliation come "through the merits, and mercy, and grace of the Holy Messiah" (2 Nephi 2:8), through the mediation of Jesus. Through the atoning blood of Christ, shed in Gethsemane and on Golgotha, we may be forgiven of our sins and enjoy the peace and comfort of the Holy Ghost once again (Mosiah 4:1–3). Through the Atonement, we are ransomed from the devil and death and hell and endless torment (2 Nephi 9:10–12), bought with a price, "with the precious blood of Christ, as of a lamb without blemish and without spot" (1 Peter 1:19). Thus we are a peculiar, a purchased, people. The worth of souls is great because an infinite price has been paid; the

Lord our Redeemer gave himself for us—he suffered death in the flesh and thereafter rose from the dead unto immortality and eternal life, thus making the same blessings available to us (D&C 18:10–16).

In addition to forgiveness of sin, the Atonement makes available the sanctification of our heart, the purging of our motives and desires. That is, we may be cleansed not only from sin but also from the effects and the pull of sin (Mosiah 5:2; Alma 13:12). Joseph Smith taught that deliverance from spiritual death comes not through education alone, not through a social gospel or ethical programs; rather, men and women must be changed, renewed, brought back to life spiritually, born again. "The Son of God came into the world to redeem it from the fall," he taught. "But except a man be born again, he cannot see the kingdom of God. This eternal truth settles the question of all men's religion. A man may be saved, after the judgment, in the terrestrial kingdom, or in the telestial kingdom, but he can never see the celestial kingdom of God, without being born of water and the Spirit. . . . He can never come unto Mount Zion, and unto the city of the living God, the heavenly Jerusalem, and to an innumerable company of angels; to the general assembly and Church of the Firstborn, which are written in heaven, and to God the judge of all, and to the spirits of just men made perfect, and to Jesus the Mediator of the new covenant, unless he becomes as a little child, and is taught by the Spirit of God."[10]

Redeemed man is man who has partaken of the powers of Christ through the Atonement, repented of his sins, and been renewed through the Sanctifier, who is the Holy Ghost. The Holy Ghost is the midwife of salvation. He is the agent of the new birth, the sacred channel and power by which men and women are changed and renewed, made into new creatures. This new birth, which comes in process of time, brings membership in the family of God: such persons are redeemed from the Fall, reconciled to the Father through the Son, made worthy of the designation of sons and daughters of God. They come to see and feel and understand things which the spiritually inert can never know. They become participants in the realm of divine experience.

A significant part of the "restitution of all things" (Acts 3:21) was the revelation to Joseph Smith concerning the nature of man. We know from the scriptures of the Restoration and from prophetic utterances that man is a dual being. On the one hand, "man is spirit" (D&C 93:33), an offspring of Deity, one who has unlimited eternal possibilities. Truly, man was created as a spirit a little lower than the Elohim, the Gods (Psalm 8:5, note 5a). On the other hand, man is housed in flesh and is the rightful inheritor of a fallen nature, a nature subject to desires, appetites, and passions. Thus "we are called mortal beings because in us are the seeds of death, but in reality we are immortal beings, because there is also within us the germ of eternal life. Man is a dual being, composed of the spirit which gives life, force, intelligence and capacity to man, and the body which is the tenement of the spirit and is suited to its form, adapted to its necessities, and acts in harmony with it, and to its utmost capacity yields obedience to the will of the spirit."[11] The spirit, joined with the body, constitutes the soul of man (D&C 88:15), and it is the redemption of the soul, not just the body, that is accomplished through the sufferings and death and rise to glory of the Holy One of Israel. For "spirit and element, inseparably connected," in the resurrection, "receive a fulness of joy" (D&C 93:33).

To understand man we must understand the source from whence he sprang, for, in the words of the choice seer, Joseph Smith, "If men do not comprehend the character of God, they do not comprehend themselves."[12] At the same time, we cannot, worlds without end, effect a permanent change in our nature or save ourselves from death and hell. Our growth in spirituality, our climb up the divine mountain, may entail a choice on our part, but it is a choice to be changed by our Divine Redeemer through his Holy Spirit. As we acknowledge our weakness, recognize our own spiritual blindness, and consider ourselves "fools before God" without divine assistance (John 9:39–41; 2 Nephi 9:42; Ether 12:27), we thereby open ourselves to a transcendent power.

NOTES

1. Rasmussen, *Lord's Question,* 4.
2. *Teachings of the Prophet Joseph Smith,* 158; see also 181.
3. *Teachings of the Prophet Joseph Smith,* 352–54.
4. Clark, *Messages of the First Presidency,* 4:203, 205.
5. Snow, *Journal of Discourses,* 14:300; see also 302.
6. Young, *Journal of Discourses,* 2:255–56.
7. *Teachings of the Prophet Joseph Smith,* 30; see also 26–27.
8. Taylor, *Mediation and Atonement,* 197; see also McConkie, *Promised Messiah,* 244, 349–50.
9. Young, *Journal of Discourses,* 12:104.
10. *Teachings of the Prophet Joseph Smith,* 12.
11. Smith, *Gospel Doctrine,* 14.
12. *Teachings of the Prophet Joseph Smith,* 343.

CHAPTER 2

WASHED IN THE BLOOD

F OUNDATIONAL TO CHANGE, renewal, rebirth, and transformation of the human character is the central verity of all eternity, the atoning sacrifice of the Lord Jesus Christ. Had there been no atonement—no matter the nobility of our desires or the tenacity of our work—nothing else we could have done on our own would have made up for that lack. Truly, as Lehi taught Jacob, "there is no flesh that can dwell in the presence of God, save it be through the merits, and mercy, and grace of the Holy Messiah" (2 Nephi 2:8).

In speaking of the role of Christ as the Mediator, Elder Boyd K. Packer declared: "Truth, glorious truth, proclaims there is . . . a Mediator. Through Him mercy can be fully extended to each of us without offending the eternal law of justice. This truth is the very root of Christian doctrine. You may know much about the gospel as it branches out from there, but if you only know the branches and those branches do not touch that root, if they have been cut free from that truth, there will be no life nor substance nor redemption in them."[1] No matter the doctrine, practice, or principle that we teach, if it is not somehow grounded in the atonement of Christ, it will have no life, no staying power. We can ascend to greater spiritual heights only to the degree that we focus on the fundamental reality of Jesus Christ and him crucified.

There is a dimension of the atonement of Christ that perhaps has not received the attention we might have given it, a doctrine taught perhaps most forcefully in the writings of the apostle Paul. We speak a great deal, and appropriately so, about how Jesus Christ *died* for us. Equally important, though, and often overlooked, is the eternal verity that Christ desires to *live* in us.

We must strive to do good and live the righteous life but seek at the same time to get beyond simply going through the motions. We have all met people who just go through the motions. Each of us has surely been in that camp at one time or another. We do the right things, but there is no joy in doing so. We are at every meeting; we read our scriptures; we pray regularly; we attend the temple; and we are absolutely burned out. We find little satisfaction in gospel living. Yes, we do need to do what is right, but enduring to the end is not a matter of simply holding on, white-knuckled, gritting our teeth and moving forward. Enduring to the end is intended to be a happy experience. W. Ian Thomas offers this thought: "There are few things quite so boring as being religious, but there is nothing quite so exciting as being a Christian.

"Most folks have never discovered the difference between the one and the other, so that there are those who sincerely try to live a life they do not have, substituting religion for God, Christianity for Christ, and their own noble endeavors for the energy, joy, and power of the Holy Spirit. In the absence of reality, they can only grasp at ritual, stubbornly defending the latter in the absence of the former, lest they be found with neither!

"They are lamps without oil, cars without gas, and pens without ink, baffled at their own impotence in the absence of all that alone can make man functional; for man was so engineered by God that the presence of the Creator within the creature is indispensable to His humanity. Christ gave Himself for us to give Himself to us! His presence puts God back into the man! He came that we might have life—God's life!

"There are those who have a life they never live. They have come to Christ and thanked Him only for what He did, but do not live in the power of who He is. Between the Jesus who 'was' and the Jesus who 'will be' they live in a spiritual vacuum trying with no little zeal to live for Christ a life that only He can live through them, perpetually begging for what in Him they already have!"[2]

Going through the motions has been likened to a situation in which a home is inhabited by two kinds of people, those who are absolutely deaf and those who can hear. One day, a man who can hear goes into the living room of that home, turns on the stereo and begins to listen to some enjoyable music. After a while he begins to tap his toe and snap his fingers. A man who is deaf looks in the doorway and sees the man sitting on the couch, presumably enjoying what he's doing, tapping his toe and snapping his fingers. The deaf man thinks to himself, *I wonder what in the world he's doing.* But because the man on the couch really seems to be enjoying himself, the deaf man sits down and observes him for a bit longer. Finally, the deaf man begins tapping his toe and snapping his fingers in time with the other man. The deaf man thinks, *This is not much fun, but he surely seems to be enjoying it.* Now there are two men sitting on the couch, tapping their toes, snapping their fingers, and smiling. The plot thickens when a third man (who can hear) looks in the door and sees the two men sitting there. He concludes that both men sitting on the couch, tapping their toes, and snapping their fingers are having the same experience. Yet nothing could be farther from the truth, for only one of them hears the music.[3]

Life in Christ is hearing the music. Yes, we must strive to do what is right. Yes, we should do our home and visiting teaching, visiting our families and caring for them, even when we are not eager to do so. We cannot just leave the work of the kingdom to others because we have not been changed and reborn, but that doesn't mean we must remain that way. We may change; we can change; we should change, and it is the Lord who must and will change us.

Coming unto Christ entails more than being cleansed, as important as that is. It entails being filled. We speak often of the importance of being cleansed, or sanctified, which is to have the Holy Spirit, who is not only a revelator but a sanctifier, remove filth and dross from our souls as though by fire. We refer to this process as a baptism by fire. To be cleansed is essential, but to stop there is to stop short of great blessings. It would be like finding my wife in the kitchen boiling twenty jars in a large container on the stove. I say to her, "Shauna, what are you doing?"

"Sterilizing jars," she answers.

I ask, "Why are you sterilizing the jars?"

"To get them clean."

"What are you going to do with the clean jars?"

"Put them on the counter."

"What are you going to do with them there?"

"I'm going to put them there so everyone can see just how clean they are."

"What purpose will they serve?"

"People will know we have clean jars."[4]

The fact of the matter is that the jars will serve precious little useful function, even though they are clean. To be useful, they must be filled. It is the same with us. It isn't enough to have the Lord through his Spirit cleanse us. He must fill us. That word, *fill,* is used repeatedly in scripture, especially in the Book of Mormon.

Paul writes: "I am crucified with Christ: nevertheless I live; yet not I, but Christ liveth in me: and the life which I now live in the flesh I live by the faith of the Son of God, who loved me, and gave himself for me" (Galatians 2:20). That is a new life in Christ. To the Saints in Ephesus, Paul wrote: "For by grace are ye saved through faith; and that not of yourselves: it is the gift of God: not of works, lest any man should boast. For we are his workmanship, created in Christ Jesus unto good works, which God hath before ordained that we should walk in them" (Ephesians 2:8–10). When we have been filled, the Spirit is with us, and Christ comes to dwell in us through that Spirit as he desires to do. Then our works begin to be motivated by that Holy Spirit, and they are no longer our works: they are his works.

The risen Lord said to the Nephites that there were certain things required before his church would be his Church: it had to have his name, and it must be built upon his gospel. If these two conditions were met, then the Father would "show forth his own works in it" (3 Nephi 27:5–10). How? His works are manifest through the body of Christ, through the members of the Church. The Father's Spirit motivates them to greater righteousness. It is not expected that we "go through the motions" all our lives. There can come a time when our motives, desires, and yearnings have been changed, and we begin to do the works the way God would do them and in the manner he would do them, because God has now begun to live in us through his Spirit.

Paul wrote: "Wherefore, my beloved, as ye have always obeyed, not as in my presence only, but now much more in my absence, work out your own salvation with fear and trembling." If we stop our reading there, and that's usually where we stop, we wonder about the phrase "work out your own salvation." How? There's not a person living on this earth who can literally work out his own salvation, that is, on his own. There aren't enough home teaching visits; there aren't enough cakes and pies to be delivered to the neighbors; there aren't enough prayers to be uttered for us to work out our own salvation. But Paul doesn't stop there: "For it is God which worketh in you both to will and to do of his good pleasure" (Philippians 2:12–13). The works are the Lord's works through us, and thus we are doing not our works but his works.

Through the atonement of Christ we do more than enjoy a change of behavior: we come to change our very nature. "Therefore if any man be in Christ, he is a new creature: old things are passed away; behold, all things are become new" (2 Corinthians 5:17). Isn't that what King Benjamin was being taught by the angel—that the natural man is an enemy to God and will stay that way unless and until he "yields to the enticings of the Holy Spirit"? (Mosiah 3:19). The evangelical scholar John Stott has explained: "We may be quite sure that Christ-centredness and Christ-likeness will never be attained by our own unaided efforts. How can self drive out self? As well expect Satan to drive out Satan! For we are not interested in skin-deep holiness, in a merely external resemblance to Jesus Christ. We are not satisfied by a superficial modification of behaviour patterns in conformity to some Christian subculture which expects this, commands that and prohibits the other. No, what we long for is a deep inward change of character, resulting from a change of nature and leading to a radical change of conduct. In a word we want to be *like Christ,* and that thoroughly, profoundly, entirely. Nothing less than this will do."[5]

Elder Glenn Pace put it this way: "We should all be striving for a disposition to do no evil, but to do good continually. This isn't a resolve or a discipline; it is a disposition. We do things because we want to, not just because we know we should. . . . Sometimes we overlook the fact that a spiritual transformation or metamorphosis must take place within us. It comes about through grace and by the Spirit of God, although it does not come about until we have truly repented and proven ourselves worthy. We can be guilty of being so careful to live the letter of the law that we don't develop our inner spiritual nature and fine-tune our spiritual communication to the point that we may receive sanctification and purification. My conclusion is that we will not be saved by works if those works are not born of a disposition to do good, as opposed to an obligation to do good."[6] This, of course, is what President Ezra Taft Benson meant when he taught that although the world deals in externals, the Lord works from the inside out.[7]

The Lord Jesus Christ came to earth not only to change us but to exchange with us. He creates in us a new identity. Note Philippians 3:8–9: "Yea doubtless, and I count all things but loss for the excellency of the knowledge of Christ Jesus my

Lord: for whom I have suffered the loss of all things, and do count them but dung, that I may win Christ, and be found in him, not having mine own righteousness, which is of the law, but that which is through the faith of Christ, the righteousness which is of God by faith." Paul wrote that Christ has reconciled us to the Father and has delivered unto his followers what we might term the "ministry of reconciliation." That is, our Mediator has reconciled us to the Father through the Atonement and asked us to extend those glad tidings to others. "To wit, that God was in Christ, reconciling the world unto himself, not imputing their trespasses unto them; and hath committed unto us the word of reconciliation [the gospel]. Now then we are ambassadors for Christ, as though God did beseech you by us [that is, He is working through his legal administrators to save souls]: we pray you in Christ's stead, be ye reconciled to God. For he [God the Father] hath made him [Christ the Son] to be sin for us, who knew no sin; that we might be made the righteousness of God in him" (2 Corinthians 5:18–21).

One of the eternal ironies of the Atonement is that in Gethsemane and on Golgotha our Lord and Savior, he who had never known sin and had never taken a backward step or a spiritual detour, became, as it were, the great sinner. The Lord not only changes our nature but offers to exchange natures with us. He takes the burden of sin. There is imputed to him (placed on his account) the sins of the world. He imputes to us—places on our spiritual ledger—his righteousness. People do not become perfect just by striving and striving to do the right things. They become perfect in and through Christ. Persons who qualify for the celestial kingdom are just men and women who have been "made perfect through Jesus the mediator of the new covenant, who wrought out this perfect atonement through the shedding of his own blood" (D&C 76:69). And so, our Lord comes to exchange with us and in that sense to provide for us a new identity. To baptize is not just to immerse. If we were to dip a white handkerchief into a vat of red dye, it could be said that we had baptized it—not only has the cloth been immersed in the liquid but it has now become a very different handkerchief. Its identity has been changed. Persons who are baptized into Jesus Christ learn to "walk in newness of life" (Romans 6:4).

One person described the transformation this way: "Being made into a new creation is like a caterpillar becoming a butterfly. Originally an earthbound crawling creature, a caterpillar weaves a cocoon and is totally immersed in it. Then a marvelous process takes place called metamorphosis. Finally a totally new creature—a butterfly—emerges. Once ground-bound, the creature can now soar above the earth. It now can view life from the sky downward. In the same way, as a new creature in Christ you must begin to see yourself as God sees you.

"If you were to see a butterfly, it would never occur to you to say, 'Hey, everybody! Come look at this good-looking, converted worm!' Why not? After all, it was a worm. And it was 'converted.' No, now it is a new creature, and you don't think of it in terms of what it was. You see it as it is now—a butterfly."[8]

Indeed, "the life of the flesh is in the blood: . . . for it is the blood that maketh an atonement for the soul" (Leviticus 17:11). It is not just the goodness of Jesus that saves us. It is not simply the fact that he was sinless and thus owed no debt to justice that transforms us from worldliness to spirituality.

Although his willingness to suffer in our behalf causes our hearts to swell with gratitude, yet the central message of Christianity to the world is that Jesus Christ "loved us, and washed us from our sins in his own blood" (Revelation 1:5). The Savior has redeemed us—purchased us, bought us back, "bailed us out"—through his blood (Ephesians 1:7). In the language of the Risen Lord to his American Hebrews: "And no unclean thing can enter into [God's] kingdom; therefore nothing entereth into his rest save it be those who have washed their garments in my blood, because of their faith, and the repentance of all their sins, and their faithfulness unto the end" (3 Nephi 27:19).

We do not become holy through lengthy theological discussions but by seeking for a remission of sins and by pleading to be filled with that Spirit which fills as well as sanctifies. I have come to know that there is a power beyond anything we could ever work ourselves into. We strive to do the works of righteousness, and that is how we keep our part of the covenant, but we plead all along that Christ will re-create us in his image. There is a life in Christ, a more abundant life, a restful and peaceful life. C. S. Lewis observed that this change in perspective, this growth into a new life in Christ, "is precisely what Christianity is about. This world is a great sculptor's shop. We are the statues and there is a rumour going round the shop that some of us are some day going to come to life."[9]

NOTES

1. Packer, Conference Report, April 1977, 80.
2. Cited in George, *Classic Christianity,* Foreword.
3. Cited in George, *Classic Christianity,* 152–53.
4. Similar example cited in George, *Classic Christianity,* 62.

5. Stott, *Life in Christ,* 109; italics in original.

6. Pace, *Spiritual Plateaus,* 62–63.

7. Benson, Conference Report, October 1985, 5.

8. George, *Classic Christianity,* 79.

9. Lewis, *Mere Christianity,* 140.

CHAPTER 3

PAUSING ON PLATEAUS

I HAVE BEEN CALLED A NUMBER OF times over the years to serve as a teacher in my ward. Because of what I do for a living, those callings have been a comfortable fit, one that has brought a great deal of satisfaction and enjoyment. I am thoroughly convinced that few callings in the Church can have a more lasting and meaningful effect on the lives of Church members (both teachers and students) than those associated with teaching the gospel.

By the time Shauna and I had been married for about ten years, I had taught deacons, priests, young adults, Gospel Essentials, Gospel Doctrine, family living, and teacher development classes. When we moved to Utah to fill an assignment at Brigham Young University, life took a different turn for me. I was not called to teach in Sunday School or priesthood quorums. I was not asked to serve in a quorum presidency or a bishopric or a high council. Rather, I was called to serve as the assistant Cubmaster. Being "Church broke," I accepted with a smile and indicated to the bishop that although I had never worked in such a capacity, I would give it my best shot. For the first few weeks I lived in denial, going through the motions but just knowing that this calling was obviously a stopping off point, an intermediate labor for one whose talents surely could be used more appropriately elsewhere. I went to the pack meetings and politely did what I was asked to do but no more. Looking back, I feel ashamed about the way I felt and acted; I was clearly caught up with myself and was tripping over my pride.

Providentially, my unhappiness with my calling (and, with the passing of time, the evidence that it would last a while). drove me to my knees. I knew, deep within my heart, that my attitude was all wrong, that my approach to service required a major overhaul. I pleaded with the Lord for several weeks for the spirit of my calling, to see and feel what I needed to see and feel. As time went by, I looked more and more carefully at the Cubmaster, Brother Owen. This saintly soul clearly loved the boys and was willing to do anything to help them. I marveled at the uncounted hours he spent preparing for pack meetings, attending leadership training, and simply hanging out with the boys. I was touched by the sincere devotion and commitment of the den mothers who willingly took time away from their own young families to serve the boys. In time, my hardened heart was softened, and I managed to climb into the saddle of service and enjoy what the Lord had asked me to do. And, as so often is the case, I was released soon thereafter.

I know how important Cub Scouting is for boys. That's simply not an issue with me. And I know how important it is for caring people to serve as leaders and workers in that program. In looking back on the experience, it seems clear to me that I wasn't in any way doubting the worth of the program or viewing it condescendingly. What I was doing was bristling at the suggestion that I do something different, something very different from what I had been called to do in the past. What I was doing was resisting change and fighting against the notion that I should leave my spiritual comfort zone. I was at ease teaching in the Church, serving in high councils, bishoprics, and stake presidencies; those callings were clearly more suited to my experience and disposition. But Cub Scouting? Come on! Yet through that calling I came to know that the Lord does not really want us to be completely comfortable, if in so doing we coast, relax, and stop stretching and developing.

Too often members of the Church decline to serve in a given calling because they have never done anything like it before, because their strengths lie elsewhere, or because they would feel uncomfortable in the new assignment. Nonetheless, that's what the kingdom of God is all about—men and women serving, whether or not they have specific training, aptitude, or strength. The Church is neither a factory nor a political organization in which people forevermore fill a given role or lobby for this or that job. We are led by farmers and plumbers and college presidents and art historians. We are taught by CPAs and lawyers and homemakers and custodians. That's the way it must be in the Lord's Church and kingdom. We are called upon to bend and stretch and reach and try new things. We are called upon to climb higher, to move on.

At about the time of the Tower of Babel, Jared and his people were spared the confusion of tongues and told that they would be led to the promised land we know as America. "And it came to pass that they did travel in the wilderness, and did build barges, in which they did cross many waters, being directed continually by the hand of the Lord." Later, "as they came to the sea they pitched their tents; and they called the name of the place Moriancumer; and they dwelt in tents, and dwelt in tents upon the seashore for the space of four years." Then follows a most interesting statement by Moroni, the editor of the Jaredite record: "And it came to pass at the end of four years that the Lord came again unto the brother of Jared, and stood in a cloud and talked with him. And for the space of three hours did the Lord talk with the brother of Jared, and chastened him because he remembered not to call upon the name of the Lord" (Ether 2:6, 13–14).

It is hard to imagine that the brother of Jared—clearly one of the great spiritual giants of all time, a man of profound righteousness—would be in a position to be chastened by the Lord for not praying for four years! It seems so contrary to the man portrayed in the scriptural account, one who was "redeemed from the fall," one whose faith and knowledge was of such a character that he "could not be kept from beholding within the veil" (Ether 3:13, 19; 12:20–21). This is the same man who had received high praise from Jehovah earlier: "And there shall be none greater than the nation which I will raise up unto me of thy seed, upon all the face of the earth. And thus will I do unto thee because this long time ye have cried unto me" (Ether 1:43).

Perhaps the brother of Jared was being reprimanded by the Lord not for avoiding prayer altogether but for failing to pray with the kind of energy and zeal and faith that had brought him and his people to that point in their journey. In other words, they seem to have been camping, content with where they were, settled into the coastal area, when in fact God wanted them to move on and complete their journey. The brother of Jared did repent, and he called upon the name of the

33

Lord in behalf of the Jaredites. The Lord forgave him but reminded the group that his Spirit would not always strive among them. "And the Lord said: Go to work and build, after the manner of barges which ye have hitherto built. And it came to pass that the brother of Jared did go to work" (Ether 2:15–16).

Likewise, in speaking of Lehi and his colony's use of the Liahona, Alma observed that "because those miracles were worked by small means it did show unto them marvelous works. They were slothful, and forgot to exercise their faith and diligence and then those marvelous works ceased, and they did not progress in their journey; therefore, they tarried in the wilderness, or did not travel a direct course, and were afflicted with hunger and thirst, because of their transgressions" (Alma 37:41–42). Like the brother of Jared and the Lehites, we too often fail to "cry unto the Lord" in the sense of seeking his mind and will, striving to find new ways to accomplish his purposes, and going to work to achieve his ends. We get comfortable. We get content. We even get lazy. We pause on life's plateaus for too long. We lose our spiritual momentum and eventually our interest in climbing higher. Too many times young men and women return from full-time missionary service and spend the rest of their lives living on the memories of the "best two years of my life," coasting spiritually on the basis of what once had happened instead of building on that foundation to achieve greater heights and deeper understanding. Alma's inquiry of the people of Zarahemla is both poignant and personal: "Behold, I say unto you, my brethren, if ye have experienced a change of heart, and if ye have felt to sing the song of redeeming love, I would ask, can ye feel so now?" (Alma

5:26). In essence, the Lord is asking you and me, "What have you done for me lately?"

President Spencer W. Kimball declared: "Now, my brothers and sisters, it seems clear to me, indeed, this impression weighs upon me—that the Church is at a point in its growth and maturity when we are at last ready to move forward in a major way. Some decisions have been made and others pending, which will clear the way, organizationally. But the basic decisions needed for us to move forward, as a people, must be made by the individual members of the Church. The major strides which must be made by the Church will follow upon the major strides to be made by us as individuals." The prophet then added: "We have paused on some plateaus long enough. Let us resume our journey forward and upward."[1]

President Gordon B. Hinckley similarly counseled us to "stand a little taller, to lift our eyes and stretch our minds to a greater comprehension and understanding of the grand millennial mission of this, The Church of Jesus Christ of Latter-day Saints. This is a season to be strong. It is a time to move forward without hesitation, knowing well the meaning, the breadth, and the importance of our mission." President Hinckley added the comforting assurance that "we have nothing to fear. God is at the helm. He will overrule for the good of this work. He will shower down blessings upon those who walk in obedience to His commandments. Such has been his promise. Of His ability to keep that promise none of us can doubt."[2]

Life is not a constant vertical climb. The process of spiritual growth and maturity seems to be one of climbing, pausing for rest and refreshment and reassurance, and then resuming the climb, on and on to the top. I have a conviction that if we will seriously call upon the Lord and ask him regularly to bless us to feel what we ought to feel and see what we ought to see, we will feel the divine hand upon our shoulder, nudging us onward and upward, all the days of our lives. We will then begin to balance the divine discontent (a constant inner enticement to repent and improve) with what Nephi called "a perfect brightness of hope" (2 Nephi 31:20) and thereby find peace here and eternal reward hereafter.

NOTES
1. Kimball, Conference Report, April 1979, 114.
2. Hinckley, Conference Report, April 1995, 95.

CHAPTER 4

COMING OUT OF
THE WORLD

PRESIDENT GORDON B. HINCKLEY has warned the Latter-day
Saints about "moving to mainstream America."[1] The
people of the covenant really should be listening to different voices, thinking and acting in different ways, and looking to other sources for guidance and direction. The repeated command from him who is holy is to "go ye out from among the wicked" (D&C 38:42). "Go ye out from Babylon," the people of Zion have been directed, "be ye clean that bear the vessels of the Lord" (D&C 133:5; compare Isaiah 52:11). Further, the scriptures affirm that the friendship of the world is "enmity with God." "Whosoever therefore will be a friend of the world is the enemy of God" (James 4:4). We are to "love not the world, neither the things that are in the world. If any man love the world, the love of the Father is not in him" (1 John 2:15).

As members of the restored Church, we are striving to become holy. To be holy is to be consecrated, dedicated, devoted, devout, pure, just, good, godly.[2] As Webster's 1828

Dictionary states, "We call a man holy, when his heart is con-
formed in some degree to the image of God, and his life is reg-
ulated by the divine precepts."[3] A holy person is therefore one
who lives a life that is patterned after the Savior's, in which
divine precepts both motivate and monitor one's conduct.

We live in a day that militates against holiness, when time-
honored values are ridiculed, and when those who stand up for
basic morality are marginalized in society. It is, in fact, the day
of Satan's power, wherein evil is called good and good is called
evil, in which darkness is labeled light and light is labeled darkness (Isaiah 5:20). Because society's slouch toward Gomorrah
will persist, it is increasingly difficult to ascertain moral truth
in the world and dangerous to follow current and future trends.
We take our cues from society at our peril. Where, in a world
afflicted with creeping relativism, do we turn for standards? A
few years ago President Hinckley cited a study conducted on
the moral values of producers, directors, and writers in
Hollywood and television. The study indicated that these persons are "far less religious than the general public and 'diverge
sharply from traditional values' on such issues as abortion,
homosexual rights and extramarital sex. . . . 'This group has
had a major role in shaping the shows whose themes and stars
have become staples in our popular culture.'"[4]

Satan seeks to dull our sensitivities to sin and to confuse
our consciences. As William Wordsworth wisely observed,
"The world is too much with us."[5] Too many things an earlier
generation would have spurned and rejected as deadly to their
souls have been allowed to become part of our world. Some of
this has happened as a result of excessive tolerance or mis-
placed loyalty. Let me illustrate. A few years ago a student at
Brigham Young University asked to visit with me after class.

She had been a student of mine for two semesters of Book of Mormon, and she was, frankly, a delight to have in class. The light of the gospel radiated from her countenance. She came in to tell me good-bye. I said, "I'll see you next year, won't I?"

She shook her head. "No, I won't be coming back to BYU."

When I asked why, she said, "Brother Millet, I'm tired. No, it's more than that—I'm worn out. I haven't slept for almost a year now."

Was she tired of studying? I asked. Wouldn't a summer break do the trick? No, that wasn't it. She explained that her roommates, all returned missionaries, had their boyfriends over each night until the early morning hours.

I was stunned. "Why didn't you tell someone? Why didn't you mention it to the landlord or the bishop?"

Her answer highlights a significant problem that many in this generation face. She said, "But wouldn't that be judging them?" We then had a long, long discussion about what it meant to judge righteous judgment. I explained to her that each of us, as men and women seeking to be holy, are under obligation to make judgments every day of our lives. We must decide whether we will spend time with some people, in particular places, doing certain things. Such decisions, very much a part of making our way through the mists of darkness, are vital; our hope for eternal life depends upon our doing so.

In our day, it seems as though the most serious flaw a person can have is to be intolerant. One would rather be immoral, unclean, degenerate. But whatever else we do, we mustn't dare to be intolerant. To be sure, we must be Christian, must be understanding, must be loving and concerned, but such virtues must never cloud the issue of what is right and what is wrong, what is good and what is evil. We must not, as Elder Dallin H.

Oaks pointed out to students at BYU, allow our strengths to become our weaknesses.[6] We must not allow our tendency to be tolerant to become the very means by which vice becomes acceptable and even encouraged. If we do not stand up for some things, we will fall for almost anything.

To be aware of sins and indiscretions in our immediate setting (our home, our quorum, or our ward) and to refuse to deal properly with these things is to be dishonest and dishonorable. It is, in a sense, to condone and even enable sin. Too often we misunderstand the principle of loyalty. I am under no obligation, even as a caring friend, to be loyal to an associate who is guilty of violating the standards of the Church or the community in which we live. My primary loyalty is to God, his Son, Jesus Christ, and the leaders of the Church. Can we not see the inconsistency of attempting to be loyal to someone who is being disloyal to divine precepts or established standards of decency?

Happy is the man or woman whose thoughts are clean and pure. We need to do all in our power to control what goes into our minds. Let us use wisdom and discernment in what movies we attend, what videos we watch, what sitcoms we faithfully watch. If for no other reason than pure obedience, we should avoid R-rated movies and any others (no matter their rating) that wink at immorality or parade excessive violence. We cannot afford to gauge our viewing according to what the box office says. Very often, in fact, box office success should serve as a caution light. "Enter ye in at the strait gate," the Savior said, "for wide is the gate, and broad is the way, that leadeth to destruction, and many there be which go in thereat: because strait is the gate, and narrow is the way, which leadeth unto life, and few there be that find it" (Matthew 7:13–14).

We must give careful attention to the music we consume, the pictures that surround us, and what we view on the Internet. Thoughts are seedbeds of action. Some years ago President Dallin H. Oaks explained to BYU students: "We are surrounded by the promotional literature of illicit sexual relations on the printed page and on the screen. For your own good, avoid it. Pornographic or erotic stories are worse than filthy or polluted food. The body has defenses to rid itself of unwholesome food, but the brain won't vomit back filth. Once recorded it will always remain subject to recall, flashing its perverted images across your mind, and drawing you away from the wholesome things in life."[7]

Another matter prevents many of us from enjoying the Spirit of the Lord in our lives as we might: the tendency to live on the edge, to play percentages with God, to tempt fate, and to place ourselves in circumstances that can contribute to our spiritual undoing. There are those who want to see how far they can go without going all the way, those who want to drive as close to the edge of the cliff as possible with no intention whatever of falling, those who cunningly creep up on the flame with no intention of ever being burned, those who want to enjoy all the privileges of Babylon but at the same time keep their citizenship in Zion intact. There is no lasting happiness in such approaches to life but rather a type of moral or spiritual schizophrenia. Too many people want to be good—but not too good; others want to be bad—but not too bad. Some want to serve the Lord without offending the devil. As my colleague Brent Top once observed, one cannot dance and dine in the great and spacious building and still hold on to the iron rod; clinging to the iron rod requires both hands, as well as both heart and soul. James taught that "a double minded man is unstable in all his ways" (James 1:8). We would do well to stay as far away from sin and compromise as we can, not only to avoid evil but also the very appearance of evil (1 Thessalonians 5:22). Prevention is far, far better than redemption.

Some years ago I conducted a temple recommend interview with a man who was serving as a priesthood leader. When I asked about his moral worthiness, he answered, "Oh, I suppose I'm morally clean. I'm faithful to my wife, but I wrestle with my thoughts all the time." We spoke at some length about what things in his life needed to be jettisoned and what things might be done to invite a greater measure of light. I mentioned that I had found it deeply rewarding and extremely helpful to listen to general conference addresses and inspiring talks and beautiful, uplifting music when I traveled in the car. He agreed to try it. I didn't speak to this brother for a number of years. When we met again, he was serving as a stake president. As we visited, he commented that the suggestion made several years earlier to fill his life with greater light and truth in the manner I had proposed had proven a godsend to him and had been a turning point in his spiritual life. It was a simple investment on his part, but one that paid rich dividends.

President George Albert Smith taught: "There are two influences in the world today, and have been from the beginning. One is an influence that is constructive, that radiates happiness and builds character. The other influence is one that destroys, turns men into demons, tears down and discourages. We are all susceptible to both. The one comes from our Heavenly Father, and the other comes from the source of evil that has been in the world from the beginning, seeking to bring about the destruction of the human family. . . .

"My grandfather used to say to his family, 'There is a line of demarcation, well defined, between the Lord's territory and the devil's. If you will stay on the Lord's side of the line you will be under his influence and will have no desire to do wrong; but if you cross to the devil's side of the line one inch, you are in the tempter's power, and if he is successful, you will not be able to think or even reason properly, because you will have lost the spirit of the Lord.'

"When I have been tempted sometimes to do a certain thing, I have asked myself, 'Which side of the line am I on?' If I determined to be on the safe side, the Lord's side, I would do the right thing every time. So when temptation comes, think prayerfully about your problem, and the influence of the spirit of the Lord will enable you to decide wisely. There is safety for us only on the Lord's side of the line."[8]

The Master calls upon his disciples to take up our cross and follow him. To "take up the cross" of Christ is to deny ourselves of ungodliness and worldly lusts (JST Matthew 16:26), to rid our lives of those influences—be they music, movies, TV sitcoms, reading material, or people—that degrade or desensitize us to righteousness and the things of eternity. I have come to know that habits, particularly habits that are unworthy of a people of covenant, may be overcome only as we draw a line of demarcation in the sand of our lives and make the commitment, "Thus far and no more." The Savior explained that "that which is of God is light; and he that receiveth light, and continueth in God, receiveth more light; and that light groweth brighter and brighter until the perfect day." These instructions have been given by a gracious Lord to enable us to "know the truth, that [we] may chase darkness from among [us]" (D&C 50:24–25).

The apostle Peter wrote to the Saints scattered abroad: "Ye

are a chosen generation, a royal priesthood, an holy nation, a peculiar people; that ye should shew forth the praises of him who hath called you out of darkness into his marvellous light" (1 Peter 2:9). We ought to search out, be sensitive to, and applaud the good that is in our society. There is much that is sweet and uplifting and edifying, but if we are to qualify to go where God and angels are, we must see to it that the distance between us and the world is increasing day by day. This will come to pass as our minds and hearts are transformed by the Spirit of God, as we come to see what we ought to see, hear what we ought to hear, and feel what we ought to feel. If we live in such a way that the Holy Ghost can dwell in us, then over time our desires are educated, our judgment is refined, our conscience is sharpened. In speaking of the former-day Saints, Alma observed that they "were sanctified, and their garments were washed white through the blood of the Lamb." Note what follows: "Now they, after being sanctified by the Holy Ghost, having their garments made white, being pure and spotless before God, could not look upon sin save it were with abhorrence; and there were many, exceedingly great many, who were made pure and entered into the rest of the Lord their God" (Alma 13:11–12).

The Holy Ghost is a revelator as well as a comforter. And the Holy Ghost is a sanctifier, the means by which waywardness and rebellion and stubbornness, sin and iniquity and vice are burned out of our souls as though by fire. That sanctifying or cleansing influence can be ours as we make up our minds to do things the way the Lord would have us do them. Too many people in today's world want to go to their graves singing with gusto, "I did it my way."

A peculiar people is a purchased people. That is, we are not our own; we have been bought with a price (1 Corinthians 6:19–20). We believe that we are saved by "the merits, and mercy, and grace of the Holy Messiah" (2 Nephi 2:8), but we do not believe in cheap grace. What cost God the Father everything, even the life blood of his Only Begotten Son, cannot be treated as "a thing of naught" (1 Nephi 19:9). We are a people of covenant. We have made supernal promises, in holy places, to stand as lights to a world desperately in need of direction and focus. We are under solemn obligation to be the salt of the earth (D&C 101:39–40), to bring out the best in the world, to preserve the world from decay and destruction. Salt does not lose its savor or influence with age; salt loses its savor through mixture and contamination.

Some are carrying heavy burdens, even the burdens of sin. Satan whispers lies to them. He suggests that serious sins are between them and God, that they can work it out by themselves. He tries to convince them that it's too late, that they have gone too far, that the way back is too difficult. These are lies, lies spawned in the infernal pits by the father of lies himself. He would have them be miserable like unto himself (2 Nephi 2:18). We must never surrender ourselves to such rubbish. There is a way back. It will not be easy, but it is possible. Priesthood leaders hold the keys that will assist in lifting the heavy weight from the heart. Our Savior suits his tender mercies to our varying and specific needs (D&C 46:15), and he who knows us best will direct our priesthood leaders to know exactly how best to bless our lives.

Webster's 1828 *Dictionary* provides an additional definition of the word *holy*. To be holy is to be whole, complete, fully formed, finished. In other words, to be holy is to be perfect in the scriptural sense. No one can of himself ever, worlds without end, become perfect in this life, no longer make mistakes, no longer take a backward step. But he can become perfect in Christ. Our Divine Redeemer is complete, while each one of us is incomplete. As I come unto him, we (the Lord and I) are complete. He is whole while I am partial. Together we are whole and complete. He is finished while I am unfinished. Together we are finished. And he is perfect while I am oh, so imperfect. Together, in covenant, we are perfect. Covenant union with Christ allows him to share with me and transfer to my spiritual account his riches and his righteousness. Thus it is that the faithful learn to rely alone upon the merits of Christ, "who [is] the author and the finisher of their faith" (Moroni 6:4).

I think often of a dear friend of mine, a man I have known for more than forty years. Over the years he has lost interest in the Church and fallen into habits that rob him of the influence of the Spirit. He has wrestled with alcoholism for about twenty-five years, and whenever we have been together in recent times I have tried to encourage him to put the liquor away and get control of his life. During a fairly recent visit, I said to him, lovingly but firmly, "Bill, you've got to get control of yourself. You've lost your wife and children, you have no discipline in your personal life, and you're on the verge of losing your job. What will it take to turn you around?" Continuing, I asked, "Why don't you come back to Church with me? God is alive and well and eager to help you if you take the first step back." He looked at me through his bloodshot eyes (he was quite intoxicated at the time) and chuckled. "Come on, Bob. Get real. You've lost touch with reality!"

I pondered on his comment: "Get real!" How ironic, I thought: here my friend had spent more than the last two decades drowning himself in a substance that helped him to avoid reality, and now he suggested that I should get real. So often members of the Church who are striving to live by a higher standard than that of the world are frequently assaulted with "Get real!" It is my conviction that life on the gospel path is the only realm that is actually real; everything else is sham and façade. The reason the grass on the other side of the fence appears to be so green is because it is plastic! It is fake. It does not represent things as they really are.

God, our Heavenly Father, lives. He is the Man of Holiness (Moses 6:57). I desire with all my strength to become a holy man, to qualify one day to go where he is. I desire the same for you. Peter wrote, "As he which hath called you is holy, so be ye holy in all manner of conversation," meaning in conduct as well as in speech. "Because it is written, Be ye holy; for I am holy" (1 Peter 1:15–16; compare Leviticus 11:44).

We can put away the things of this world and become a people of purpose. We can begin to change society, one person at a time. We have the promise that "they that be with us are more than they that be with them" (2 Kings 6:16), that, as John the Beloved instructed the Saints in his day, "greater is he that is in you, than he that is in the world" (1 John 4:4). God grant that we, the people of the covenant, will be wise in the days of our probation, that we will put away the foolishness of the flesh and put out of our lives those things that have no place among a people concerned with holiness. I pray that we will do so, that we may in time see the face of the Lord with pleasure and hear those tender words of welcome, "Come unto me, ye blessed, there is a place prepared for you in the mansions of my Father" (Enos 1:27).

NOTES

1. Hinckley, Conference Report, October 1997, 93.

2. *Random House College Dictionary,* s.v. "holy."

3. *Webster's Dictionary,* 1828, s.v. "holy."

4. *Teachings of Gordon B. Hinckley,* 461–62.

5. As cited in Lyon, et al., *Best Loved Poems of the LDS People,* 305.

6. Oaks, "Our Strengths," 107–15.

7. Cited in Tanner, Conference Report, October 1973, 124.

8. Smith, *Sharing the Gospel,* 42–43.

CHAPTER 5

SEVEN-DAY-A-WEEK
HOLINESS

A GROUP OF DISSENTERS FROM the Nephites "built up in the center of their synagogue, a place for standing, which was high above the head; and the top thereof would only admit one person" (Alma 31:13). Those who climbed atop the tower, called the Rameumptom, recited a memorized prayer in which they thanked God that they were a chosen people and acknowledged their superiority over the lost and deceived ones about them. Mormon adds this poignant detail about the Zoramites: "Now, after the people had all offered up thanks after this manner, they returned to their homes, never speaking of their God again until they had assembled themselves together again to the holy stand, to offer up thanks after their manner" (Alma 31:23).

One challenge we face in our ascent to greater spiritual heights is to resist the temptation to separate our religious life from our everyday life, to be an electrician or an accountant from Monday through Saturday and a Christian on Sunday. In writing of the tendency for men and women to substitute activity for spirituality, C. S. Lewis observed that man has "sub-stituted religion for God, as if navigation were substituted for arrival, or battle for victory, or wooing for marriage, or in gen-eral the means for the end. But even in this present life, there is danger in the very concept of *religion*. It carries the suggestion that this is one more department of life, an extra department added to the economic, the social, the intellectual, the recre-ational, and all the rest. But that whose claims are infinite can have no standing as a department. Either it is an illusion or else our whole life falls under it. We have no non-religious activi-ties; only religious and irreligious."[1]

In discussing how we can enjoy a spirit of holiness throughout the week, let us first consider our responsibility to observe and honor the Lord's Sabbath. The observance of the Sabbath predates Sinai, for we learn from Moses that after the Gods had completed the paradisiacal creation of all things, the Lord "rested on the seventh day from all his work which he had made. And God blessed the seventh day, and sanctified it: because that in it he rested from all his work which God created and made" (Genesis 2:2–3; see also Moses 3:2–3). Although there is no mention in the Old Testament about the Sabbath or Sabbath observance during the times of Abraham, Isaac, and Jacob, we would suppose, knowing the import of this statute, that the former-day Saints during patriarchal times did in fact honor the seventh day as a holy memorial. From the time of the Exodus of the children of Israel from Egypt, the Sabbath commemorated the deliverance of the covenant people from bondage. "Keep the sabbath day to sanctify it, as the Lord thy God hath commanded thee. . . . And remember that thou wast a servant in the land of Egypt, and that the Lord thy God brought thee out thence through a mighty hand and by a stretched out arm: therefore the Lord thy God commanded thee to keep the sabbath day" (Deuteronomy 5:12, 15). This could mean, therefore, that the Sabbath was kept on a different day each year.

During their wilderness wanderings the Israelites were instructed to gather enough manna on the day prior to the Sabbath so that they would have sufficient. "And Moses said, Eat that to day: for to day is a sabbath unto the Lord: to day ye shall not find it in the field. Six days ye shall gather it; but on the seventh day, which is the sabbath, in it there shall be none" (Exodus 16:25–26). Indeed, the seriousness of the law of the Sabbath is illustrated in an instance in Numbers 15, in which "a man that gathered sticks upon the sabbath day" is stoned to death by the congregation of Israel (vv. 32–36).

Inasmuch as a proper observance of the Sabbath signals and symbolizes a worshipful attitude, it follows that during periods of waywardness the people of God ceased to comply with this law. Thus Nehemiah's reform included a reinstitution of a strict Sabbath observance. "In those days saw I in Judah some treading wine presses on the sabbath, and bringing in sheaves, and lading asses. . . . Then I contended with the nobles of Judah, and said unto them, What evil thing is this that ye do, and profane the sabbath day? Did not your fathers thus, and did not our God bring all this evil upon us, and upon this city? yet ye bring more wrath upon Israel by profaning the sabbath. And it came to pass, that when the gates of Jerusalem began to be dark before the sabbath, I commanded that the gates should be shut, and charged that they should not be opened till after the sabbath: and some of my servants set I at the gates, that there should no burden be brought in on the sabbath day" (Nehemiah 13:15–19).

During the centuries preceding the coming of the Messiah, efforts to interpret the Law of Moses resulted in massive commentary, rules, and "traditions of the elders." No aspect of the Law became more burdensome and cumbersome than the law of the Sabbath. Endless lists and formulae pertaining to servile work, distances to be traveled, and in general what was and was not appropriate for the Sabbath—these things constituted an integral part of daily life among Jews in the first century. "We do not overstate our case," Elder Bruce R. McConkie wrote, "when we say that the Jewish system of Sabbath observance that prevailed in the day of Jesus was ritualistic, degenerate, and almost unbelievably absurd, a system filled with fanatical restrictions."[2] In an effort to establish a sane perspective on the Sabbath day—to point up the spiritual inconsistency associated with so many innane restrictions—Jesus took occasion to lift and teach and heal and work miracles, to do good on the Sabbath, for which he was attacked by his enemies among the Jewish leaders. "Wherefore the Sabbath was given unto man for a day of rest," he taught, "and also that man should glorify God, and not that man should not eat; for the Son of Man made the Sabbath day, therefore the Son of Man is Lord also of the Sabbath" (JST Mark 2:26–27). After Jesus' mortal ministry, the members of The Church of Jesus Christ observed the first day of the week as the Sabbath day, the Lord's day, in remembrance of the resurrection of the Master (Acts 20:7; 1 Corinthians 16:2; Revelation 1:10).

Why would God stress so strongly the proper observance of the Sabbath? In a very practical way, the Sabbath was given to man to enable us to take a break, to rest our tired bodies, to renew ourselves physically. So many in our modern age work themselves to exhaustion, working long days (and even into the night) in an effort to get ahead financially and get a jump on rising costs. Too often they choose to work on the Sabbath, only to face themselves in the mirror on Monday mornings unrested and unsatisfied. The body is the temple of God (1 Corinthians 3:16–17; 6:19), and we can do ourselves quite as much harm through overwork as we can by other more obvious forms of abuse.

Perhaps more important than our need for physical respite is our need for spiritual rest. Many of us face the world Monday through Saturday in a hostile environment that tugs at our testimony and digs at our devotion. We engage a fallen world that weakens our resolve and entices us toward ungodliness. The Sabbath is fundamentally necessary to charge our batteries and empower our souls. President Brigham Young noted that "the Lord has planted within us a divinity; and that divine, immortal spirit requires to be fed. Will earthly food answer for that purpose? No. It will only keep this body alive as long as the spirit stays within it." President Young also explained, "That divinity within us needs food from the Fountain from which it emanated."[3] "It is a day of worship," President Joseph F. Smith declared, "a day in which the spiritual life of man may be enriched. A day of indolence, a day of physical recuperation is too often a very different thing from the God-ordained day of rest. . . .

" . . . A proper observance of the duties and devotions of the Sabbath day will, by its change and its spiritual life, give the best rest that men can enjoy on the Sabbath day."[4]

It is essential for us to go to church to participate in those sacraments or ordinances that provide a clear channel for divine power. "And that thou mayest more fully keep thyself unspotted from the world," Jesus said in a modern revelation, "thou shalt go to the house of prayer and offer up thy sacraments upon my holy day; for verily this is a day appointed unto you to rest from your labors, and to pay thy devotions unto the Most High" (D&C 59:9–10). Partaking of the sacrament of the Lord's Supper enables us to renew sacred covenants—our promise to take the Lord's name, to keep his commandments, to bear one another's burdens—and to renew the Lord's promise to us—that we can be forgiven and renewed in spirit, that we may always have his Spirit to be with us (Moroni 4–5).

Partaking of the sacrament allows us to cleanse our souls of sin, revive our spirits, and renew our quest for holiness. Elder Melvin J. Ballard asked: "Who is there among us that does not wound his spirit by word, thought, or deed, from Sabbath to Sabbath? We do things for which we are sorry and desire to be forgiven, or we have erred against someone and given injury. If there is a feeling in our hearts that we are sorry for what we have done, if there is a feeling in our souls that we would like to be forgiven, then the method to obtain forgiveness is not through rebaptism; . . . it is to repent of our sins, to go to those against whom we have sinned and transgressed and obtain their forgiveness and then repair to the sacrament table where, if we have sincerely repented and put ourselves in proper condition, we shall be forgiven, and spiritual healing will come to our souls. It will really enter into our being."[5]

President David O. McKay emphasized the value of the sacramental service in allowing us a period of deep reflection and introspection. "Here is an opportunity to commune with oneself and to commune with the Lord. We meet in the house that is dedicated to Him; we call it the Lord's house. Well, you may rest assured that He will be there to inspire us if we come in proper attune to meet Him."[6]

There is a grander sense in which proper Sabbath observance rests our souls. Too many of us depend upon church attendance and weekly association with the Saints to make all the difference in our spiritual lives; we suppose that one-day-a-week holiness is sufficient to make it through the mists of darkness. I am persuaded that the Sabbath serves us most powerfully when we have earnestly sought through the week to come unto Christ—through at least daily efforts at personal and family devotion. One reason we often have such difficulty pondering on the Savior and his atoning sacrifice during the sacramental service is that we have not thought much about such things Monday through Saturday. On the other hand, when we are striving to think and ponder and pray and search the scriptures during the week, then the Sabbath becomes a capstone to a well-spent week. It is of such seven-day-a-week holiness that the Master speaks when he says, "Nevertheless thy vows shall be offered up in righteousness on all days and at all times" (D&C 59:11).

Several years ago, when I was teaching the Gospel Doctrine class in our ward, my wife Shauna and I were trying to decide whether we should go to a particular movie one Saturday evening. We had heard that it was quite good, but we also knew that it was rated PG-13 and that there were some objectionable parts. I finally said to Shauna, "Let's don't go. I have to teach Gospel Doctrine class in the morning, and I don't want to do anything that would keep me from enjoying the Spirit of the Lord." So we talked and read for a few hours that night.

As I laid my head on the pillow at about 11:00 P.M., I reflected on what a noble choice I had made, on how

55

wonderful it was that I had exercised the appropriate restraint. And then there came some unanticipated thoughts: "So you think you're really something, huh? Well, what if this had been a Tuesday night or a Thursday night? Would you still have been as concerned about tarnishing your mind and heart? Would you have gone to the movie then, or do you plan to go next Wednesday or Friday?" My smug self-righteousness was rapidly transformed into the remorseful realization that ours is a seven-day-a-week religion and that I should be just as concerned about what I consume on Monday morning as I am on Saturday night. My vows, meaning my covenants, made at baptism and in the holy temple, should and must guide me throughout the entire week.

The scriptures often speak of *rest* in other ways as well. The Sabbath is a day of rest, a day wherein we seek to enter the "rest of the Lord," that is, "rest from doubt, from fear, from apprehension of danger, rest from religious turmoil of the world."[7]

To rest on the Sabbath is also to move closer to that supernal day when we are permitted to enter God's presence (JST Exodus 34:1–2) and receive the fulness of his glory (D&C 84:24). We thus rest here, in this life, in preparation for the ultimate rest hereafter. Mormon declared, "Wherefore, I would speak unto you that are of the church, that are the peaceable followers of Christ, and that have obtained a sufficient hope by which ye can enter into the rest of the Lord, from this time henceforth until ye shall rest with him in heaven" (Moroni 7:3).

The Sabbath allows us to focus, at least once a week, on matters of eternal import. We are all expected to cultivate the spirit of revelation and the spirit of Christian service every day of our lives, but the Sabbath provides us a unique opportunity to divorce ourselves from the cares of Babylon—making money, meeting deadlines, competing—and give our full time and attention to the establishment of Zion. On the Sabbath we teach our families the gospel, study the scriptures and the words of the living oracles, and in general delight in the things of the Spirit. To observe the Sabbath, President Spencer W. Kimball wrote, "one will be on his knees in prayer, preparing lessons, studying the gospel, meditating, visiting the ill and distressed, sleeping, reading wholesome material, and attending all the meetings of that day to which he is expected."[8] President Harold B. Lee explained that "Sunday is more than a day of rest from the ordinary occupations of the week. It is not to be considered as merely a day of lazy indolence and idleness or for physical pleasures and indulgences. It is a feastday for your spirit bodies."[9]

Because the Lord established the Sabbath as a day of rest at the consummation of the Creation, it would be wise for us to reflect, on the Sabbath, on the goodness and omnipotence of our Creator, to ponder on the beauties and wonders about us. Because the Sabbath at one time in history commemorated the deliverance of ancient Israel from the hold of the Egyptians, it would be wise for us on the Sabbath to reflect on the power of the Almighty's arm to deliver us from ignorance and sin and death and eternal unhappiness. Because—since the ministry of the Messiah—the Sabbath has pointed us to his rise from death, it would be wise for us to reflect, on the Sabbath, on the infinite and eternal atoning sacrifice of Jesus the Christ. President David O. McKay observed: "Our Sabbath, the first day of the week, commemorates the greatest event in all history—Christ's resurrection, and his visit as a resurrected being to his assembled Apostles."[10] Elder Mark E. Petersen added that "our observance or nonobservance of the Sabbath is an unerring measure of our attitude toward the Lord personally and toward his suffering in Gethsemane, his death on the cross, and his resurrection from the dead. It is a sign of whether we are Christians in very deed, or whether our conversion is so shallow that commemoration of his atoning sacrifice means little or nothing to us."[11]

The leaders of the Church have made it abundantly clear that God expects a covenant people to be true to their covenants, including our ongoing promise to observe the Sabbath properly. We cannot expect to avoid the perils that await the ungodly if we are contributors to society's ungodliness and irreverence. Elder George Albert Smith declared the following in a much quieter and more reverent day than our own: "The Sabbath has become the play-day of this great nation, the day set apart by thousands to violate the commandment that God gave long, long ago, and I am persuaded that much of the sorrow and distress that is afflicting and will continue to afflict mankind is traceable to the fact that they have ignored his admonition to keep the Sabbath day holy."[12] President Spencer W. Kimball stated: "I again would urge upon all Saints everywhere a more strict observance of the Sabbath day. The Lord's holy day is fast losing its sacred significance throughout the world, at least our world. More and more, man destroys the Sabbath's sacred purposes in pursuit of wealth, pleasure, recreation, and the worship of false and material gods."[13] He also said: "Brethren and sisters, once again I call to our attention the fourth commandment given by the Lord to Moses on Mount Sinai. . . . Let us observe it strictly in our homes and in our families. Let us refrain from all unnecessary labors. Sunday is not a day for hunting and fishing, nor for swimming, picnicking, boating, or engaging in any other sports."[14]

President Ezra Taft Benson said, "I don't believe that it is possible to keep our spirituality on a high plane by spending our Sabbaths on the beach, on the golf course, in the mountains, or in our own homes reading newspapers and looking at television. When the Lord said, 'And that thou mayest more fully keep thyself unspotted from the world, thou shalt go to the house of prayer' (D&C 59:9), that is exactly what He meant. We must have spiritual food.

"Of course you can live a pretty good life out on the golf course on Sunday. But you don't build your spirituality. Probably you could worship the Lord out there, but the fact is you don't do it as you don't worship him down on the beach. But if you go the house of the Lord you will worship him. If you attend to your prayers in your home with your family you will worship him. And your spirituality will be raised. The spiritual food which your body requires will be provided and you will be much more apt to have this joy."[15]

"We note," President Kimball observed, "that in our Christian world in many places we still have business establishments open for business on the sacred Sabbath. We are sure the cure of this lies in ourselves, the buying public. Certainly the stores and business houses would not remain open if we, the people, failed to purchase from them. Will you all please reconsider this matter. Take it to your home evenings and discuss it with your children. It would be wonderful if every family determined that henceforth no Sabbath purchase would be made."[16]

"I wish I had the power," President Gordon B. Hinckley said, "to convert this whole Church to the observance of the

Sabbath. I know our people would be more richly blessed of the Lord if they would walk in faithfulness in the observance of the Sabbath. . . . There isn't anybody in this Church who has to buy furniture on Sunday. There really isn't. There isn't anybody in this Church who has to buy a new automobile on Sunday, is there? No. There isn't anybody in this Church who, with a little care and planning, has to buy groceries on Sunday. . . . You don't need to make Sunday a day of merchandising. . . . I don't think we need to patronize the ordinary business merchants on the Sabbath day. Why do they stay open? To get customers. Who are those customers? Well, they are not all nonmembers of this Church. You know that and I know that."[17]

Note the counsel from President James E. Faust: "Over a lifetime of observation, I have noticed that the farmer who observes the Sabbath day seems to get more done on his farm than he would if he worked seven days. The mechanic will be able to turn out more and better products in six days than in seven. The doctor, the lawyer, the dentist, or the scientist will accomplish more by trying to rest on the Sabbath than if he tries to utilize every day of the week for his professional work. I would counsel all students, if they can, to arrange their schedules so that they do not study on the Sabbath. If students and other seekers after truth will do this, their minds will be quickened and the infinite Spirit will lead them to the verities they wish to learn. This is because God has hallowed his day and blessed it as a perpetual covenant of faithfulness."[18]

We live in a rapidly decaying world, in a society that is taking the most direct route to destruction. Because we cannot afford to partake of worldliness, we must seek to do all in our power to acquire and cultivate holiness. "Be ye holy," we have been told, "for I [the Lord] am holy" (1 Peter 1:16; see also

Leviticus 11:44). More specifically, "Ye shall keep my sabbaths, and reverence my sanctuary: I am the Lord" (Leviticus 19:30). "But remember that on this, the Lord's day, thou shalt offer thine oblations and thy sacraments unto the Most High, confessing thy sins unto thy brethren, and before the Lord. And on this day thou shalt do none other thing, only let thy food be prepared with singleness of heart that thy fasting"—that is, our hungering and thirsting after righteousness—"may be perfect, or, in other words, that thy joy may be full. Verily, this is fasting and prayer, or in other words, rejoicing and prayer" (D&C 59:12–14).

One sign and witness to God and to all men and women that we are eager to keep ourselves unspotted from the vices of the world is our willingness to keep the Sabbath day holy. It is a token of holiness, a visible symbol of our desire to honor Jehovah, even him who established the Sabbath. If we strive daily to draw near unto God—through even brief but consistent scripture study, pondering, and prayer—the Sabbath will indeed become the spiritual highlight and capstone of our week, the culmination of a diligent quest for holiness and peace. We thereby qualify for the cleansing and motivating power of the Holy Spirit in our lives and thus enter into the rest of the Lord. The Holy One becomes our God, and we become his people, a people of covenant.

NOTES
1. Lewis, *Letters to Malcolm,* 30; italics in original.
2. McConkie, *Mortal Messiah,* 1:201.
3. Young, *Journal of Discourses,* 7:138.
4. Smith, *Gospel Doctrine,* 242.
5. Ballard, *Melvin J. Ballard,* 132–33.
6. McKay, *True to the Faith,* 231–32.
7. Smith, *Gospel Doctrine,* 58.

8. Kimball, *Miracle of Forgiveness,* 97.

9. *Teachings of Harold B. Lee,* 210.

10. McKay, *Gospel Ideals,* 397–98.

11. Petersen, Conference Report, April 1975, 72.

12. Smith, Conference Report, October 1935, 120.

13. Kimball, Conference Report, October 1978, 5.

14. Kimball, Conference Report, October 1979, 4.

15. *Teachings of Ezra Taft Benson,* 439.

16. Kimball, Conference Report, October 1975, 6.

17. As cited in Tingey, Conference Report, April 1996, 11–12.

18. Faust, *Finding Light in a Dark World,* 112.

CHAPTER 6

DAY OF DECISION

THE NATURAL MAN—the unregenerated man, the fallen man, the man whose first priority is self—fights tenaciously to establish his own will and agenda. Thus, as someone has observed, "fallen man is not simply an imperfect creature who needs improvement: he is a rebel who must lay down his arms."[1] On the other hand, disciples of Christ, at a certain point in their spiritual climb, make a huge discovery and an equally huge resolve—they realize that the Lord can do so much more with their lives than they can, and so they determine to do things the Lord's way.

Sometimes we are like the poverty-stricken Zoramites in the Book of Mormon who were compelled to be humble (Alma 32:13–16). That is, only after some of us have tried things our way for a season and failed miserably do we sense a better and more productive way—the Lord's way. I have come to know firsthand some of the despondency and guilt associated with falling short of my goals, of trying to do it all, of striving to make myself perfect. The apostle Paul seems to have been addressing a similar problem in his day. He wrote: "Brethren, my heart's desire and prayer to God for Israel is, that they might be saved. For I bear them record that they have a zeal of God, but not according to knowledge. For they being ignorant of God's righteousness, and going about to establish their own righteousness, have not submitted themselves unto the righteousness of God. For Christ is the end of the law for righteousness to every one that believeth" (Romans 10:1–4).

I suspect that many Latter-day Saints will agree to the same faulty orientation I find occasionally in myself. My greatest frustrations seem to come as a result of my efforts to "handle it" myself, or, in other words, my failure to trust in and rely on the Lord. Maybe it's our culture that contributes to our dilemma; maybe it's the constant chants of "You can do anything you put your mind to," or "You have unlimited possibilities and potential" that tend to focus our attention away from the powers of the divine toward *our* abilities, *our* merits, and *our* contributions. I have come to know that the answer to our problems is not to be found alone in humanity, no matter how impressive our accomplishments.

Few things in this life are exactly as they seem to be. We live in a time, for example, where everyone is told of the importance of being in control. We must be in charge. We must have access to and management over all the variables. We operate by plans and formulae and procedures. Lists and tables and charts abound. One of the harsh realities facing someone acclimated to this fallen world is that spiritual things are not programmable. We cannot require or demand or shape spiritual experience. The Spirit is in control, not us. The Lord through his Spirit works his marvelous wonders in his own time, in his own way, and according to his own will and purposes. To enter the realm of divine experience, therefore, is to enter a realm where we are not in complete control. We can seek to be worthy, strive to be in a position to be blessed, plead and pray for divine intervention, but we do not force the hand of the Almighty.

Though such qualities as self-reliance and self-confidence may prove valuable in some of our dealings in this life, the reciprocal principles of submission, surrender, and having an eye single to the glory of God are essential if we are to acquire that enabling power described in scripture as the saving grace of Jesus Christ. It is as if the Lord inquires of us: "Do you want to be a possessor of all things such that all things are subject unto you?" We, of course, respond in the affirmative. He then says: "Good. Then submit to me. Yield your heart unto me." The Lord asks further: "Do you want to have victory over all things?" We nod. He follows up: "Then surrender to me. Unconditionally." Odd, isn't it? We incorporate the powers of divinity only through acknowledging our own inabilities, accepting our limitations, and realizing our weakness. We open ourselves to infinite strength only through accepting our finite condition. We in time gain control only through being willing to relinquish control.

Too much of my own frustration over the years has come as a result of my refusal to let go and thus let God. Something— I suppose it is the natural man, the prideful self that automatically asserts its own agenda—drives me to want to do it myself. Oh, I believe in God, to be sure, that he loves me, that he sent his Son to earth to help me. All too often, however, my actions have betrayed my limited orientation, my vision of Christ as a type of spiritual advisor, a sort of celestial cheerleader who stands on the sidelines and whispers encouragement, rather than the Lord God Omnipotent who came to earth to make men and women into new creatures through empowering them to do what they could never do for themselves.

One Christian writer observed: "God is not only our orchestrator, but our composer. Christ Jesus is the author and *finisher* of our lives. (See Hebrews 12:2.) As long as we insist on writing our own stories, he cannot write his living will onto our hearts. As long as we insist on forging our own paths, he cannot lead us into his paths of righteousness. As long as we insist on governing our own lives, he cannot be our sovereign King and Lord. As long as we insist on living life according to our own desires, he cannot impart his desires or guide us into his wholeness, fruitfulness, and blessings. As long as we feel that we are in control of our fate, we cannot experience fully the destiny he has for us. We are *his* workmanship. When we act otherwise, we are breaching our trust relationship with God and are refusing to submit our lives fully to him."[2]

Elder Boyd K. Packer taught a profound lesson many years ago. "I knew what agency was," he said, "and knew how important it was to be individual and to be independent, to be free. I somehow knew there was one thing the Lord would never take from me, and that was my free agency. I would not surrender my agency to any being but to Him! I determined that I would *give* Him the one thing that He would never take—my agency. I decided, by myself, that from that time on I would do things His way.

"That was a great trial for me, for I thought I was giving away the most precious thing I possessed. I was not wise enough in my youth to know that because I exercised my agency and decided myself, I was not *losing* it. It was *strengthened!*"[3] In a leadership meeting a number of years ago, Elder

Packer spoke, very soberly, of that time in his life when he had determined to surrender his agency to God. He then recommended to the priesthood leaders that we consider doing the same but added, with unaccustomed sternness, "But don't you monkey with this. This is serious business!"

And indeed it is. We really should not offer something if we have no intention of letting it go. We really should not indicate to the Almighty that we intend to give him everything when in fact we are prepared to give him only a small portion. There's a rather frightening story in Acts 5 about a man and his wife who ostensibly consecrated their all to the Lord through the apostles, but in reality they "kept back" a portion of their goods, just in case their stewardship or inheritance was not sufficient for their desires. Both Ananias and his wife, Sapphira, died suddenly. "And great fear came upon all the church, and upon as many as heard these things" (Acts 5:11).

Now, to be sure, the Lord seldom strikes people down because of their duplicity, but this story demonstrates powerfully that the Master expects us to be honest about our offering. In fact, what can we offer to God? Our savings accounts? Our properties? Our investments? No, for he already owns all of this world's goods. "The earth is the Lord's, and the fulness thereof; the world, and they that dwell therein" (Psalm 24:1). As Elder Neal A. Maxwell pointed out, "The submission of one's will is really the only uniquely personal thing we have to place on God's altar. The many other things we 'give,' brothers and sisters, are actually the things he has already given or loaned to us. However, when you and I finally submit ourselves, by letting our individual wills be swallowed up in God's will, then we are really giving something to Him! It is the only possession which is truly ours to give! Consecration thus constitutes the only unconditional surrender which is also a total victory!"[4]

After describing the premortal war in heaven, John the Revelator wrote: "And I heard a loud voice saying in heaven, Now is come salvation, and strength, and the kingdom of our God, and the power of his Christ; for the accuser of our brethren [Satan] is cast down, which accused them before our God day and night. For they have overcome him by the blood of the Lamb, and by the word of their testimony; for they loved not their own lives, but kept the testimony even unto death. Therefore, rejoice O heavens, and ye that dwell in them" (JST Revelation 12:9–11). In that same spirit, the Lord commended Nephi, the son of Helaman, for his faithfulness: "Blessed art thou, Nephi, for those things which thou hast done; for I have beheld how thou hast with unwearyingness declared the word, which I have given unto thee, unto this people. And thou hast not feared them, and hast not sought thine own life, but hast sought my will, and to keep my commandments. And now, because thou hast done this with such unwearyingness, behold, I will bless thee forever; and I will make thee mighty in word and in deed, in faith and in works; yea, even that all things shall be done unto thee according to thy word, for thou shalt not ask that which is contrary to my will" (Helaman 10:4–5). If we in time will seek to align ourselves with God's will, he will in eternity grant unto us whatsoever we ask, for our desires will have been educated and our hearts purified of selfishness. If we here submit, we shall there inherit. As C. S. Lewis wisely observed, "There are really only two kinds of people in the end: those who say to God, 'Thy will be done,' and those to whom God says, in the end, 'Thy will be done.'"[5]

It is true that praying "Thy will be done" may entail

submitting to difficult or challenging circumstances ahead. C. S. Lewis provided a slightly different approach to this scripture: "'Thy will be done.' But a great deal of it is to be done by God's creatures; including me. The petition, then, is not merely that I may patiently suffer God's will but also that I may vigorously do it. I must be an agent as well as a patient. I am asking that I may be enabled to do it. . . .

"Taken this way, I find the words have a more regular daily application. For there isn't always—or we don't always have reason to suspect that there is—some great affliction looming in the near future, but there are always duties to be done; usually, for me, neglected duties to be caught up with. 'Thy will be *done*—by me—now' brings one back to brass tacks." Further, Lewis explained, "Thy will be done" may also imply a readiness on our part to receive and experience new and unanticipated blessings. "I know it sounds fantastic," he added, "but think it over. It seems to me that we often, almost sulkily, reject the good that God offers us because, at that moment, we expected some other good."[6] "Thy will be done" thus represents our petition that the Almighty work his wonders through us, that he soften our hearts to new ideas, new avenues of understanding, and open us to new paths and new doors of opportunity when it is best for us to move in another direction.

Most Latter-day Saints agree with what has been said to this point. That is, each of us knows, deep down within us, that eventually we must surrender to the Lord and open ourselves to his will for us. But not today. Not now. Not that way. Surely, we suppose, there will come a time when we will be more prepared to make the sacrifice of self and to lay it all on God's altar. But not now. About the time I turned eighteen years of age, I was deeply involved in the activities and programs of the

Church. I was a stake missionary, had memorized some of the missionary discussions and scriptures, and proselyted with the full-time missionaries at least a couple of nights per week. I was so excited about serving a full-time mission that I couldn't wait for the time to pass when my bishop (who was my dad) and I could begin the paperwork and interviews. All was well for several months, and then, without warning, my attitudes and my ideas began to change. I gradually began to think more and more about life at home, about friends and school, and about how long two years really was. In looking back now on that season of my life, there's no question but that Satan began to make subtle inroads into my character and my resolve to be a missionary.

I remember my father sitting down with me on a number of occasions about the time of my nineteenth birthday and asking, "Well, son, shall we begin the process?" I recall an answer that went something like, "Look, I really do want to do this, but I just don't feel prepared yet. I'm not quite ready." This happened at least three times. The last time my dad heard those words about my lack of readiness he gently and lovingly said, in effect, "Robert, this is your decision. It's something you need to do on your own. You need to pray sincerely about this. Your mom and I will never pressure or push you to go on a mission." And then he added this pertinent comment: "But let me say one more thing. You're as ready as anyone I know. If you wait until you are perfectly prepared to go, you will never go."

Likewise, if we wait until some special, red-letter day to offer our all to the Almighty, the day may never come. "Indeed," Elder Neal A. Maxwell has reminded us, "one of the most cruel games anyone can play with self is the 'not yet' game—hoping to sin just a bit more before ceasing; to enjoy the praise of the world a little longer before turning away from the applause; to win just once more in the wearying sweepstakes of materialism; to be chaste, but not yet; to be good neighbors, but not now. One can play upon the harpstrings of hesitations and reservations just so long, and then one faces that special moment—a moment when what has been sensed, mutely, suddenly finds voice and cries out with tears, 'Lord, I believe; help thou mine unbelief.' (Mark 9:24.)

"The truth is that 'not yet' usually means 'never.' Trying to run away from the responsibility to decide about Christ is childish. Pilate sought to refuse responsibility for deciding about Christ, but Pilate's hands were never dirtier than just after he had washed them.

"The past of each of us is now inflexible. We need to concentrate on what has been called 'the holy present,' for now is sacred; we never really live in the future. The holy gift of life always takes the form of now. Besides, God asks us now to give up only those things which, if clung to, will destroy us!

"And when we tear ourselves free from the entanglements of the world, are we promised a religion of repose or an Eden of ease? No! We are promised tears and trials and toil! But we are also promised final triumph, the mere contemplation of which tingles the soul."[7]

In short, is there a better day than today? Will there be a better time to repent, a more appropriate or fitting occasion for improvement or refinement or commitment? Or will we make today a moment that matters, an instant in eternity toward which we will look back with gratitude and thanksgiving for a decision that counted? Truly, as Amulek declared, "now is the time and the day of [our] salvation; and therefore, if [we] will repent and harden not [our] hearts, immediately shall the great

71

plan of redemption be brought about unto [us]" (Alma 34:31; compare 2 Corinthians 6:2).

In the first estate, the premortal world, the great Jehovah declared, "Father, thy will be done, and the glory be thine forever" (Moses 4:2). In Gethsemane, as the hours of atonement began, he said in prayer, "Not my will, but thine, be done" (Luke 22:42; compare Matthew 26:39; Mark 14:36). As he breathed his last breath on the accursed cross of Calvary, Jesus said, as the capstone to his incomparable life: "Father, it is finished, thy will is done." He then "yielded up the ghost" (JST Matthew 27:54). That sacred submission—coupled with his divine inheritance from the Eternal Father—is what made him who he was. That sublime relinquishment of will enabled him to do what no other mortal could do. That quest to know the will of the Father and then follow it opened him to incomprehensible powers of God. There is a lasting lesson here for us. Spiritual growth takes place as we become more and more willing to submit, more and more anxious to learn and carry out the will of him who knows best what to do with us. Through divine grace and assistance (D&C 109:44), we are enabled to see things as they really are, to realize what really matters, and to consecrate our whole souls toward the realization of God's great work and glory, "to bring to pass the immortality and eternal life of man" (Moses 1:39).

NOTES
1. Lewis, *Mere Christianity,* 59.
2. Stanley, *Blessings of Brokenness,* 36–37; italics in original.
3. Packer, Conference Report, April 1976, 47; italics in original.
4. Maxwell, Conference Report, October 1995, 30.
5. Lewis, *Great Divorce,* 72.
6. Lewis, *Letters to Malcolm,* 25–26.
7. Maxwell, Conference Report, October 1974, 16.

CHAPTER 7

CHOOSING THAT GOOD PART

I T IS SO VERY EASY IN TODAY'S BUSY and complex world to get caught up in the thick of thin things, to become prey to the less important. Programs and procedures begin to take priority over principles and even over people. Means begin to occupy us more than ends. Making a living, being included in the best social circles, providing the family with nice cars, lovely clothes, or extravagant travel opportunities—these may make life more enjoyable and more comfortable, but they are not necessarily the stuff out of which eternal happiness is made. Life is a mission, not a career. We come here to gain experience and to acquire the attributes of godliness. At least as important as knowledge and experience and spiritual growth is *relationships*. We have been sent to earth to learn to live together in love, to build and perpetuate the family unit. Indeed, the family is one of the few things that will continue into the eternities.

People matter more than things. People matter more than schedules and timetables and products. God and Christ work full-time in the business of people, and perhaps that primary labor contributes measurably to their fulness of joy. Sometimes when the more important things get crowded out by the less important, the Lord finds a way to jolt us back to reality and focus us on fundamentals. Occasionally that refocusing comes through the staggering confrontation with death, the stark realization that we are here on earth for only a brief season. Often it comes through what we call tragedy—an injury, a crippling disease, a terrible trauma. And once in a while it comes through incidents much less dramatic but equally direct. To paraphrase the Savior, what does it profit us if we gain the whole world and then—because of neglect or distraction—forfeit the eternal associations that bring the deepest feelings of fulfillment?

Many years ago I sat on the floor in front of a small bookcase in the dining room of our family's tiny, two-bedroom apartment. I was immersed in reading and referencing and marking in the process of preparing a book for publication. Deadlines were crowding in on me. Ironically, I was perusing President David O. McKay's book *Gospel Ideals,* when Angela, my eldest daughter, then two and a half, walked over to me and asked me to join her, one-year-old David, and my wife, Shauna, in some games they were playing on the floor about twenty feet away. I responded to Angie that I was very busy and couldn't make it. Within three minutes David crawled over and asked, "Dad, you come play?" I called out to my wife at that point, "Shauna, can't you see that what I am doing is important? Could you please keep these children out of my hair until I finish this project?"

I dived into my research. But then I felt my attention being drawn back to my wife and my children, almost as if I were being turned about physically. I looked into three sets of eyes and what I saw was not very settling—there was hurt, and in Shauna's eyes, at least, a bit of frustration. Then a voice came into my mind. Whether it was the voice of the Holy Ghost or the voice of conscience, I don't know: it was nevertheless an inner awareness of my duty. It stated simply but boldly: "Brother, behold the plan of salvation!" In that brief instant there came a rush of feelings—feelings of perspective, for in a flash I saw and felt things as they really were; feelings of overwhelming love for a trusting wife and adorable children; and yes, feelings of guilt for neglecting the most important people in my life. A rapidly repentant father crawled over to his family and became involved in things that really matter. In the years since that experience, I have reflected again and again on what I felt that evening.

Maybe it was the consuming love for my family, combined with a spiritual slap in the face, that awakened me momentarily. Other things over the years have served a like function. Shauna has gotten my attention occasionally when I have chosen to bury myself in a book and ignore the family. She has said simply, "Bob, if you're not careful, you may grow up to be a very learned ministering angel!" That works too! I haven't always been the greatest husband and father since that red-letter day in my life, but I have been better. And it is amazing how we can be tutored by the medium of memory.

Sometimes only the Lord can tell us what matters most at a given time. To both John Whitmer and Peter Whitmer Jr. the Lord explained that "the thing which will be of the most worth unto you will be to declare repentance unto this people, that you may bring souls unto me, that you may rest with them in the kingdom of my Father" (D&C 15:6; 16:6). Elder Bruce R.

McConkie stated: "I am fully aware of the divine decree to be actively engaged in a good cause; of the fact that every true principle which works for the freedom and blessing of mankind has the Lord's approval; of the need to sustain and support those who espouse proper causes and advocate true principles—all of which things we also should do in the best and most beneficial way we can. The issue, I think, is not *what* we should do but *how* we should do it; and I maintain that the most beneficial and productive thing which Latter-day Saints can do to strengthen every good and proper cause is to live and teach the principles of the everlasting gospel.

"There may be those who have special gifts and needs to serve in other fields," he continued, "but as far as I am concerned, with the knowledge and testimony that I have, there is nothing I can do for the time and season of this mortal probation, that is more important than to use all my strength, energy and ability in spreading and perfecting the cause of truth and righteousness, both in the Church and among our Father's other children."[1]

Repeated emphasis by our leaders on simplification and reduction of Church programs is surely a call to prioritize, to focus on fundamentals, to emphasize things that matter most. Even being totally involved in the programs and auxiliaries of the Church does not exempt us from sifting through the mounds of noble enterprises out there and concentrating on what is of most worth at a given time. We can be so busy, for example, in doing "Church work" that we fail to immerse ourselves in the enterprises that lead to personal holiness and thus to the deepest fulfillment in life. "Too many of us," President Boyd K. Packer stressed, "are like those whom the Lord said '[came] with a broken heart and a contrite spirit, . . . [and] at the time of their conversion, were baptized with fire and with the Holy Ghost, *and they knew it not.'*

"Imagine that: 'And they knew it not.' It is not unusual for one to have received the gift and not really know it.

"I fear this supernal gift is being obscured by programs and activities and schedules and so many meetings. There are so many places to go, so many things to do in this noisy world. We can be too busy to pay attention to the promptings of the Spirit."[2]

One of the most beloved of biblical stories is found at the end of the tenth chapter of the Gospel of Luke. Jesus and his disciples arrive in a town, presumably Bethany, and are welcomed by Martha into her home, the home shared with her brother Lazarus and her sister Mary (JST John 11:1–2). We are told that Mary "sat at Jesus' feet, and heard his word. But Martha was cumbered about much serving, and came to him, and said, Lord, dost thou not care that my sister hath left me to serve alone? Bid her therefore that she help me. And Jesus answered and said unto her, Martha, Martha, thou art careful and troubled about many things: but one thing is needful: and Mary hath chosen that good part, which shall not be taken away from her" (Luke 10:38–42).

As we know, this episode has been used in a variety of ways to teach an endless array of lessons. Let me point us in a direction that has especial relevance to this discussion. Here's the scene: Martha is in the kitchen making meal preparations for what may well have been a large number of persons. She is obviously honored that the Master and his disciples have chosen to visit, and so, like any normal hostess, wants the occasion to be as pleasant and enjoyable as possible. Martha therefore proceeds on a major production, supposedly a large, multicourse meal. While her thought to provide a feast for the Savior and his company is commendable, Martha's time-consuming efforts tend to remove her from conversation with the Christ. Her sister Mary, on the other hand, seems less concerned with preparing and providing food and more concerned with feasting on the Bread of Life.

Before we travel too far in our discussion of this story, it is important that we acknowledge that Martha is a good woman, a devoted disciple of the Lord Jesus Christ. It seems unfair to speak, as some Christians have done over the generations, of Martha as the perfect hostess and of Mary as the perfect disciple. To borrow a Book of Mormon allusion, it could probably be said of Martha that she "was not a whit behind" her sister in terms of faithfulness and dedication (see Helaman 11:19). Later in the Gospels, at the time of the death of her brother Lazarus, Martha will hear the immortal words of Jesus: "I am the resurrection, and the life: he that believeth in me, though he were dead, yet shall he live: and whosoever liveth and believeth in me shall never die. Believest thou this?" Martha's powerful witness and response follow: "Yea, Lord: I believe that thou art the Christ, the Son of God, which should come into the world" (John 11:25–27). She is solid, and her testimony is sure. Further, as one commentator has observed, "All her anxiety was to provide suitable and timely entertainment for our Lord and His disciples. And we should not, on the merest supposition, attribute earthly-mindedness to a woman whose character stands unimpeachable in the gospel."[3] But there is a lesson or two that Martha needed to learn, a lesson that each of us needs desperately to incorporate as well.

The scriptural account states that Martha was "cumbered about much serving." That is, she was burdened, worried, full of cares, distracted from learning from the Lord because of where she had chosen to expend her effort. One Evangelical Protestant minister has explained that the good she "was doing for Jesus had distracted her from Jesus. I mean if you were to ask Martha what she was doing, there was not sin involved. She wasn't disobeying God, she was just over-involved. Her calendar had become filled with cooking, not fellow-shipping with the Savior. . . .

"My question to you today is: How many good things are you doing that are keeping you away from an intimate relationship with God? I am talking about good things. . . . [Martha] comes out and she accuses the Lord, Jesus Christ, of not caring. Very important point here, folks. Don't blame God for the distractions in your life if He is not your highest priority. . . . [T]he problem wasn't either the Lord or her sister. Martha's problem was Martha. . . .

"Now you know what [the Lord] was telling us? Change your menu. Very important: change your menu. 'Martha, if cooking a banquet for me is going to keep you away from me, cook a casserole. If doing good things for me, . . . things that are not sin, things that are all okay to do, if those things are going to keep you away from me, then let's get some peanut-butter sandwiches. Remember why you invited me to your house Martha? You invited me, because you wanted the Master inside. What good is the Master inside if you never get to be with the Master?"[4]

Jesus instructed Martha—and all of us—that "one thing is needful: and Mary hath chosen that good part, which shall not be taken away from her" (Luke 10:42). In a practical vein, only one dish was needed at this gathering, clearly because overmuch preparation precluded participation in the gospel discussion. In a broader sense, the "one thing" that is forevermore needed by each and every soul is to receive the word of the Lord. "Priority is given to the hearing of the word coming from God's messenger over preoccupation with all other concerns. Martha wanted to honor Jesus with an elaborate meal, but Jesus reminds her that it is more important to listen to what he has to say. The proper 'service' of Jesus is attention to his instruction, not an elaborate provision for his physical needs."[5]

Truly, the word of God, which comes either directly from him or through his anointed servants, is more powerful than anything else when it comes to leading people to do that which is just (Alma 31:5), when it comes to the creation and enrichment of faith in the hearts of men and women (Romans 10:17). "Yea, we see that whosoever will may lay hold upon the word of God, which is quick and powerful, which shall divide asunder all the cunning and the snares and the wiles of the devil, and lead the man of Christ in a strait and narrow course across that everlasting gulf of misery which is prepared to engulf the wicked—and land their souls, yea, their immortal souls, at the right hand of God in the kingdom of heaven, to sit down with Abraham, and Isaac, and with Jacob, and with all our holy fathers, to go no more out" (Helaman 3:29–30).

There is a more subtle lesson to be learned from Mary and Martha concerning how we view our brothers and sisters. Catherine Corman Parry has observed about this episode in Luke: "Those of us with more of Martha than of Mary in us have long felt that [Jesus'] rebuke is unjust. While we do not doubt the overriding importance of listening to the Lord, does the listening have to be done during dinner preparations? Would it have hurt Mary to have joined us in serving, then we all could have sat down to hear the Lord together? And furthermore, what about the value of our work in the world? If it weren't for us Marthas cleaning whatever we see and fussing over meals, there would be a lot of dirty, hungry people in this world. We may not live by bread alone, but I've never known anyone to live without it. Why, oh, why couldn't the Lord have said, 'You're absolutely right, Martha. What are we thinking of to let you do all this work alone? We'll all help, and by the way, that centerpiece looks lovely?

"What [Jesus] did say is difficult to bear, but perhaps somewhat less difficult if we examine its context. . . . The Lord did not go into the kitchen and tell Martha to stop cooking and come listen. Apparently he was content to let her serve him however she cared to, until she judged another person's service: 'Lord, dost thou not care that my sister hath left me to serve alone? Bid her therefore that she help me' (v. 40). Martha's self-importance, expressed through her judgment of her sister, occasioned the Lord's rebuke, not her busyness with the meal."[6]

In general, the story of Mary and Martha is a story about priorities, about where we will and should place our emphasis and direct our attention. It forces us to ask hard questions about how we spend our time in the planning of Church functions or the preparation or delivery of lessons. One Young Women's advisor shared several letters she had received from some of the young women in her class. They were expressions of appreciation for her efforts in their behalf. One note said: "I enjoyed the camps and the fun activities, but most of all I loved your lessons. They touched my heart, strengthened my testimony, and have done more than anything else to motivate me to live a faithful life." The advisor sighed and expressed her frustration about so much time being taken up each week with what she called "cute" activities—birthday celebrations, spot-lights, and the planning of outside events—that she seldom has more than ten to fifteen minutes on any given Sunday to teach a gospel lesson.

What's wrong with this picture? Stated simply, we can get so caught up with the peripherals, with the external stuff of the Church (programs, procedures, policies, activities) that we lose sight of what things make the most difference in people's lives. To be sure, activity and social interaction are important parts of Church programs, but they are the something extra that makes the main course even better. We must never forget what comes first.

Our time on earth is a stewardship from God, our Heavenly Father. To the extent that we "improve our time" (Alma 34:33), choose "that good part" of life which will "not be taken away from [us]" (Luke 10:42), we are able to climb the mountain of spirituality and mature into that holiness to which he who is most holy has called us.

NOTES
1. McConkie, Conference Report, October 1973, 55; italics in original.
2. Packer, Conference Report, April 2000, 8; italics in original.
3. *Clarke's Commentary,* 872.
4. Evans, "Priority of Worship," n. p.
5. Fitzmyer, *Gospel According to Luke,* 892.
6. Parry, "'Simon, I Have Somewhat to Say,'" 116.

CHAPTER 8

CONSCIOUSNESS OF VICTORY OVER SELF

MANY YEARS AGO I ACCEPTED an assignment in the Church Educational System as a coordinator of seminaries and institutes in the eastern United States. I was a little uncertain about my duties, so I was especially happy to be invited to the first training session for all of the coordinators. Because the large group of us were so spread about the country, it was nice to get to know everyone, to compare notes, and to gain specific direction from our supervisor. I was impressed with all my colleagues but especially with one of the youngest in the group. He possessed a quiet dignity, a composure and a wisdom unusual for his age and relative inexperience. As luck would have it, we were assigned to room together at the conference.

That evening after the meetings, the two of us talked in our motel room about many things, especially about our families, our backgrounds, and gospel topics. At 2:30 A.M. we agreed— knowing that our first meeting was quite early—it was time for sleep. We had prayer together and then on our own, and I turned off the light above my bed. My colleague's light was still on, and he was sitting on the foot of his bed reading. I asked him what he was doing. "I'm just reading my scriptures for a few moments," he answered.

"It's almost three o'clock in the morning," I responded. "Why don't you go to bed and read a little extra tomorrow?"

"No," he said. "I need to spend a few moments in the scriptures and then I'll go to bed." I pressed him (insensitively, I now realize) until he explained, rather reluctantly, that he always read his scriptures for a few moments each day, that he had not missed a day in eleven years, and that it was very important to him to be able to take care of that before closing the day in sleep. I lay in bed for some time reflecting on what I had just heard and, more importantly, what I felt. Obviously, I was impressed with his accomplishment and his personal discipline, but there was more: I sensed that the gravity of his words and the wisdom of his conversation reflected his doctrinal depth and his unwearying resolve to engage the things of the Spirit daily. That experience took place nearly twenty-five years ago. Recently I spoke with one of his children, who explained that, to his knowledge, his father has not missed a day of scripture study in the intervening years. What a commitment! What a life!

My friend possessed more than knowledge, more than insight into scripture, and even more than personal discipline as a result of his daily regimen. His wasn't just a feeling of accomplishment associated with achieving a goal; he was enjoying the fruits of keeping a covenant, a covenant to center his attention upon things of greatest worth. His rather remarkable achievement had developed within him a quiet but powerful confidence, an inner awareness that he was heading in the right direction, that his life was in order. President David O. McKay explained that "spirituality is the highest acquisition of the soul, 'the divine in man—the supreme crowning gift that makes him king of all created things.' It is the consciousness of victory over self, and of communion with the Infinite. To acquire more and more power, to feel one's faculties unfolding, and one's soul in harmony with God and with the Infinite— that is spirituality. It is that alone which really gives one the best in life."[1]

It is interesting that President McKay stated that spirituality is the *consciousness* of victory over self. It is not just that we have overcome a habit, stuck with a resolve, or performed a difficult but necessary task. It is that we know we have done so. The Prophet Joseph Smith taught that three things are essential for any rational and intelligent being to exercise faith in God unto life and salvation: First, the idea that God actually exists; second, a correct idea of his character, perfections, and attributes; and third, an actual knowledge that the course in life one is pursuing is according to the will of God.[2] The first two prerequisites for faith depend upon our knowledge of God— who he is and what he is like. The third depends upon us— our own knowledge or assurance that what we are doing is pleasing God. In other words, it is one thing to have confidence in God (which a knowledge of his nature and his divine attributes brings), and quite another to feel the divine sanction and approbation of our own lives that come through the whisperings of the Holy Spirit.

Let me illlustrate from scripture. "In those days was Hezekiah [king of Judah] sick unto death. And Isaiah the prophet the son of Amoz came unto him, and said unto him, Thus saith the Lord, Set thine house in order: for thou shalt die, and not live." One might be prone to say at that point, "Thanks so much for dropping by, Isaiah. I could have gone all day without that comforting message!" But Hezekiah, one of the few righteous kings in Judah's history, "turned his face toward the wall, and prayed unto the Lord, and said, Remember now, O Lord, I beseech thee, how I have walked before thee in truth and with a perfect heart, and have done that which is good in thy sight." Then "Hezekiah wept sore." There is a sweet boldness, a quiet confidence manifest in Hezekiah's prayer; while he certainly knew that he was not perfect—and his petition was addressed to an all-powerful and all-righteous Being—he expressed the deepest desires and longings of his heart, no doubt borne of many years of fruitful service and faithful obedience to God and his laws. He could pray in confidence because his life was in order. And what was the result? "Then came the word of the Lord to Isaiah, saying, Go, and say to Hezekiah, Thus saith the Lord, the God of David thy father, I have heard thy prayer, I have seen thy tears: behold, I will add unto thy days fifteen years" (Isaiah 38:1–5).

Hezekiah's was a prayer of faith, a prayer that evidenced deep spirituality, a humble consciousness of victory over self. He had tried his best to be faithful, to be true to God, and he knew it. His experience suggests an analogy. Let's take two young Latter-day Saint couples, newly married, all students in college, struggling to make ends meet. Suppose they find themselves faced with the choice of paying their tithing or buying groceries for the week. Let's complicate the picture by suggesting that they have no family or relatives nearby to whom they might appeal for aid and no intention of asking the bishop for assistance. One couple, after some discussion, concludes, "Well, we need to be smart. The Lord certainly expects us to use our heads, to be rational about the matter. He expects us to eat, to stay alive, doesn't he? It seems that the wise course is to buy food. We can always catch up on our tithing in the next few months."

Let's try now to imagine their prayer together that evening before retiring. "Heavenly Father," they begin, "we have made a decision to do the smart thing. We know thou dost not expect us to be foolish or to go hungry, and so we have purchased groceries. We will make up for the tithing we owe later. Now, we'd appreciate any help thou couldst send us. We really do need thy help."

Contrast that prayer with one offered by the other couple, whose priorities were slightly different and who chose to pay their tithing and then trust in the divine promises: "Heavenly Father, we need thy help. We have done as thou hast asked us to do: we have paid our tithing, and so now we have no money for food. Wilt thou please open the windows of heaven and, as thou hast promised, pour out a blessing upon us that will enable us to meet our obligations? We have sought to keep the law upon which that blessing is predicated."

This is a prayer of faith, a prayer that evidences, first of all, the couple's confidence in that God who declared, "I, the Lord, am bound when ye do what I say; but when ye do not what I say, ye have no promise" (D&C 82:10). In addition, the prayer evidences a measure of confidence in themselves that strengthens their ability to live by faith and exercise a lively hope in good things to come. "Let us therefore come boldly unto the throne of grace, that we may obtain mercy, and find grace to help in time of need" (Hebrews 4:16; compare Moses 7:59).

Why do we fast? What is the purpose of fasting? Certainly as Latter-day Saints our monthly fast provides a marvelous opportunity for us to care for the poor and needy through a generous fast offering. It represents our effort, through established priesthood channels, to take of our abundance and impart unto those in need, according to what the scriptures call "the law of [the] gospel" (D&C 104:18).[3] Jehovah asked ancient Israel, "Is [the proper fast] not to deal thy bread to the hungry, and that thou bring the poor that are cast out to thy house? when thou seest the naked, that thou cover him; and that thou hide not thyself from thine own flesh?" (Isaiah 58:7).

Some six months before his death, the Savior, accompanied by his disciples, returned from the magnificent experience on the Mount of Transfiguration. A man came to Jesus and pleaded in behalf of his son who was possessed by an evil spirit. The man added, "I brought him to thy disciples, and they could not cure him." Jesus scolded the people for their unbelief, cast out the devil himself, summoned them to greater faith, and stated, "Howbeit this kind goeth not out but by prayer and fasting" (Matthew 17:14–21).

What does fasting do to enhance faith and prayer? In one sense, we demonstrate to the Lord that we are serious about obtaining divine assistance when we fast; that is, our self-denial is a manifestation of our willingness to put our own satisfaction on hold in order to obtain the power and help of the Almighty. We thus fast "to loose the bands of wickedness, to undo the heavy burdens, and to let the oppressed go free"— to "break every yoke." In other words, we fast for spiritual strength, for remission of sins, to have the burdens of waywardness lifted from our souls. As taught in modern revelation, we fast to demonstrate to the Lord our yearning for deeper spirituality, our hunger and thirst after righteousness, to grow in joy and rejoicing (D&C 59:13–14).

We strengthen ourselves spiritually as we choose to weaken ourselves physically; we gain in inner strength as we become masters of our appetites and passions, as we deny our physical selves. We grow in spirituality not just as we gain victory over ourselves but as we become conscious of doing so. President McKay thus observed, "If there were no other virtue in fasting but gaining strength of character, that alone would be sufficient justification for its universal acceptance."[4]

As a full-time missionary a few decades ago, I watched with much interest (and sadness) as a few of the elders struggled to keep the mission rules. One guideline that was particularly difficult for some was arising at the proper time each morning. It was my experience that those who chose to sleep in never quite caught the spirit of the mission; they seemed to be running behind spiritually most of the time. I find the same thing to be true today in my own life. It is not particularly difficult for me to get up in the morning at the proper time, especially since I have obligations at my place of employment—classes to teach, meetings to attend, and so forth. The real discipline for me is going to bed on time in order to be properly rested when I do arise the next morning. It only takes a few days of too little sleep to be out of sorts physically and dull spiritually. My mind and my heart—and thus my capacity to know the mind and heart of Deity—depend upon proper physical rest.

Some years ago I worked with a young man who had been guilty of serious transgression and who was under Church discipline. I met with him often and discussed each time his spiritual progress. To be honest, over a period of several months after the disciplinary council I couldn't discern much progress. He attended his Church meetings, prayed each day, read the scriptures, and did all the other things we generally associate with being active in the Church. But his heart wasn't changing. Finally, I asked him to describe his typical day. He did so and then described his typical night. He indicated that most evenings he started playing video games not long after dark and continued to do so until about three or four o'clock in the morning. I then knew what the problem was. This young man lacked the kind of personal discipline and commitment that lead to deepened spirituality and a closeness to the Spirit. To be sure, he wasn't viewing pornography or even questionable movies, just wasting his time and dissipating his physical, emotional, and spiritual resources.

In speaking to BYU students, Elder Boyd K. Packer said: "I have learned that the best time to wrestle with major problems is early in the morning. Your mind is then fresh and alert. The blackboard of your mind has been erased by a good night's rest. The accumulated distractions of the day are not in your way. Your body has been rested also. That's the time to think something through very carefully and to receive personal revelation.

"I've heard President Harold B. Lee begin many a statement about matters involving revelation with an expression something like this: 'In the early hours of the morning, while I was pondering upon that subject,' and so on. He made it a practice to work on the problems that required revelation in the fresh, alert hours of the early morning.

"The Lord knew something when He directed in the Doctrine and Covenants, 'Cease to sleep longer than is needful; retire to thy bed early, that ye may not be weary; arise early, that your bodies and your minds may be invigorated' (D&C 88:124). . . .

"I counsel our children to do their critical studying in the early hours of the morning when they're fresh and alert, rather than to fight the physical weariness and mental exhaustion at night. I've learned that the dictum 'Early to bed, early to rise' is powerful. When under pressure—for instance, when I was preparing this talk—you wouldn't find me burning the midnight oil. Much rather I'd be early to bed and getting up in the wee hours of the morning, when I could be close to Him who guides this work."[5]

I have found that one of the most difficult things to do is to establish a life that is balanced—to be faithful without being obnoxious, to have certitude without arrogance, to be tolerant without being spineless. I have found it especially difficult to be happy and joyous, to be sociable and to have a healthy sense of humor, without losing control of my emotions and becoming light-minded. Obviously the Holy One of Israel is offended when we speak lightly of sacred things, profane the holy in a spirit of jest, or become vulgar or crude in our humor. Consider what may happen in social gatherings when the hour is late, the mood light, our bodies and minds weary, and thus our emotional and spiritual restraints weakened. Before long something may be said that causes a ripple of laughter, followed by more jokes and more and deeper laughter. Within a short time our emotional and spiritual control may be seriously threatened.

Something deep down inside of us whispers that this is not good, that there is something inappropriate about loud laughter and light-mindedness. And that's exactly what the Lord said to the Latter-day Saints. After having instructed the early Saints in regard to honoring the Sabbath, he counseled: "And inasmuch as ye do these things with thanksgiving, with cheerful hearts and countenances, not with much laughter, for this is sin, but with a glad heart and a cheerful countenance—verily

I say, that inasmuch as ye do this, the fulness of the earth is yours" (D&C 59:15–16). In the revelation we know as the Olive Leaf, the Master likewise instructs us to "cast away your idle thoughts and your excess of laughter far from you." He goes on to direct, "Therefore, cease from all your light speeches, from all laughter, from all your lustful desires, from all your pride and light-mindedness, and from all your wicked doings" (D&C 88:69, 121). The warning against "light speeches" and "light mindedness" is a statement of divine concern regarding vanity or treating lightly the things of God, which vanity brings condemnation (D&C 84:54–55). While no people in all the wide world have more to be grateful for than the Latter-day Saints, while no one should be happier and more elated to be alive than the Latter-day Saints, yet there are limits of propriety in the outward expression of our joy, for "that which cometh from above is sacred, and must be spoken with care, and by constraint of the Spirit; and in this there is no condemnation" (D&C 63:64).

At the closing session of his first general conference as president of the Church, President Harold B. Lee lovingly but firmly counseled the Church regarding the excess of laughter in a general conference meeting: "I wonder sometimes if we forget that all we say in this sensitive building is going out over the air from a sacred assembly. It doesn't mean that we should be long-faced, should not show our joy, but we ought to couch our expressions of joy not with the audible expression that swells up to a great crescendo that might be mistaken by those who are listening on the outside. I think it would be well for us to remember that, with a sense of our responsibility to the most high God."[6]

Finally, there is one additional area of required victory

worth mentioning briefly. It has to do with our speech, with what proceeds from our mouths. It is quite amazing to notice that many who would never consider stealing or cheating or being immoral have little or no difficulty making biting comments or finding fault or belittling another. A personal story will help to make the point and also demonstrate my own struggles with this matter. Only a short time ago my mother, who lives in Louisiana, came to visit my family for a week. On Saturday evening I made some comment about all of us going to church together the next morning. My mother, who wrestles courageously with a number of physical maladies, indicated that she would certainly make it to sacrament meeting but wasn't certain, because of some of her challenges, how long she would be able to stay at church. Without thinking—including without remembering all that she had taught me through the years, including the faithfulness and dedication in the Church she and my father had demonstrated in my younger years—I said: "Well, Mom, going to all three meetings is what active members of the Church do!" I knew the moment the words left my mouth that they went into her heart like a dagger. She quietly bowed her head and said she would do her best.

In the hours and days that followed my insensitive and arrogant comment, I hurt all over. I had insulted my sweet mother in the presence of her daughter-in-law and her grandchildren, and, more painfully, I had belittled a person who had given of herself for a long time. She wasn't worthy of that kind of treatment. It was a sin of the heart that evidenced to me, ever so clearly, that I am not as far along as I thought I was, for in the poignant words of the Savior, "out of the abundance of the heart the mouth speaketh" (Matthew 12:34). We talked about my blunder a few days later, I apologized profusely, and she, of course, forgave me. But the damage was done, and the pointed words could not be called back.

Because of this episode I was driven to reread the words of James, the brother of our Lord. "If any man among you," he wrote, "seem to be religious, and bridleth not his tongue, but deceiveth his own heart, this man's religion is vain" (James 1:26). Truly, "the tongue is a fire, a world of iniquity" (James 3:6). I understand ever so much more clearly now that "the tongue can no man tame; it is an unruly evil, full of deadly poison. Therewith bless we God, even the Father; and therewith curse we men, which are made after the similitude of God. Out of the same mouth proceedeth blessing and cursing. My brethren, these things ought not so to be" (James 3:8–10). I have found myself, more and more, praying not only for forgiveness for my unruly tongue but also pleading to be cleansed and purified to such extent that I, first of all, bite my tongue and thus guard my speech. I hope against hope that eventually I will reach the point of spiritual maturity wherein I feel no desire whatsoever to make hurtful comments. It is a struggle of a lifetime, an ongoing battle to put off the natural man and put on Christ.

Before he emigrated from Great Britain to the United States, Charles W. Penrose was called to serve a mission in Birmingham, England. He took with him several items of furniture that might be used in the home. After some ten years of difficult but faithful service, Elder Penrose gathered up the furniture he had taken with him and prepared to depart. One elder supposed that Elder Penrose was taking things that did not belong to him and so spread the word. This hurt Elder Penrose deeply. His character and integrity had been brought into question. He had been wrongfully accused. In deep sorrow and spiritual distress, he sat down and penned the following poem, which is now one of my favorite hymns:

School thy feelings, O my brother;
Train thy warm, impulsive soul.
Do not its emotions smother,
But let wisdom's voice control.
School thy feelings; there is power
In the cool, collected mind.
Passion shatters reason's tower,
Make's the clearest vision blind.

School thy feelings; condemnation
Never pass on friend or foe,
Though the tide of accusation
Like a flood of truth may flow.
Hear defense before deciding,
And a ray of light may gleam,
Showing thee what filth is hiding,
Underneath the shallow stream.

Should affliction's acrid vial
Burst o'er thy unsheltered head,
School thy feelings to the trial;
Half its bitterness hath fled.
Art thou falsely, basely slandered?
Does the world begin to frown?
Gauge thy wrath by wisdom's standard;
Keep thy rising anger down.

Chorus:
School thy feelings, O my brother;
Train thy warm, impulsive soul.
Do not its emotions smother,
But let wisdom's voice control.[7]

Elder Boyd K. Packer spoke of a lesson he learned from an elderly woman he had been assigned to visit as a young man. "She said she wanted to tell me something and that I was always to remember it. Then began the lesson I have never forgotten. She recounted something of her life.

"A few years after her marriage to a fine young man in the temple, when they were concentrating on the activities of young married life and raising a young family, one day a letter came from 'Box B.' (In those days a letter from Box B in Salt Lake City was invariably a mission call.)

"To their surprise they were called as a family to go to one of the far continents of the world to help open the land for missionary work. They served faithfully and well, and after several years they returned to their home to set about again the responsibilities of raising their family.

"Then this little woman focused in on a Monday morning. It could perhaps be called a blue washday Monday. There had been some irritation and a disagreement; then some biting words between husband and wife. Interestingly enough, she couldn't remember how it all started or what it was over. 'But,' she said, 'nothing would do but that I follow him to the gate, and as he walked up the street on his way to work I just had to call that last biting, spiteful remark after him.'

"Then, as the tears began to flow, she told me of an accident that took place that day, as a result of which he never returned. 'For fifty years,' she sobbed, 'I've lived in hell knowing that the last words he heard from my lips was that biting, spiteful remark.'

"This was the message to her young home teacher. She pressed it upon me with the responsibility never to forget it. I have profited greatly from it."[8]

We are sent to earth to gain a physical body, live in a fallen world, and eventually bring our mind and heart and physical being into the level of submission that allows us access to divine strength. There is power in overcoming. There is majestic power in conquering. There is consummate power in gaining the victory over ourselves. And there is a quiet confidence in that consciousness of victory over self that brings peace and assurance. On the one hand, we can choose to yield ourselves to the devil and simply allow things to take their own course. In pursuing such a path, we surrender to the enemy of all righteousness and eventually forfeit our freedom. "He that hath no rule over his own spirit is like a city that is broken down, and without walls" (Proverbs 25:28). On the other hand, we can choose to turn to the Lord of hosts and gain strength to overcome. "Pray always, that you may come off conqueror; yea, that you may conquer Satan, and that you may escape the hands of the servants of Satan that do uphold his work" (D&C 10:5). The choice is ours.

NOTES

1. McKay, *True to the Faith*, 244–45.
2. Smith, *Lectures on Faith*, 3:2–5.
3. Romney, *Ensign*, January 1973, 99.
4. McKay, *True to the Faith*, 81.
5. Packer, "Self-Reliance," 356–57.
6. Lee, Conference Report, October 1972, 176.
7. *Hymns*, no. 336.
8. Packer, *Let Not Your Heart Be Troubled*, 187–88.

CHAPTER 9

COMMUNION WITH THE INFINITE

N O PERSON ASCENDS THE mountain of spirituality who does not lift his voice and his heart in prayer to the Almighty. We remember President David O. McKay's definition of spirituality: "Spirituality is the consciousness of victory over self, and of communion with the Infinite."[1]

Why do we pray? First, we believe our Heavenly Father is a Man of Holiness (Moses 6:57), a glorified and exalted Being to be sure, but a resurrected and redeemed Man who is literally the Father of our spirits. He knows us, one by one, and has infinite love and tender regard for each one of us. He has a physical body, parts, and passions. He feels. He yearns. He pains and sorrows for our struggles and our wanderings. He delights in our successes. He responds to petitions and pleadings. He is neither untouchable nor unapproachable. Thus our prayers allow us to express to God our needs, our challenges, our deepest feelings and desires, and to ask sincerely for his help. The more prayerful we become, the more dependent we are upon God and thus the more trusting and reliant upon spiritual powers beyond our own. Prayer thus builds our spiritual strength by pointing us beyond our limited resources to him who has all power. In short, we pray to better understand who we are and who God is. We pray to better understand what we can do on our own and what we can do only with divine assistance.

Second, prayer allows us to communicate with Deity, to open ourselves to conversation with divinity. If indeed the quality of our lives is largely a product of the kinds of associations we enjoy, then we may rest assured that individuals who spend much time in prayer will in time blossom in personality, rise above pettiness, littleness of soul, and mortal jealousies and fears. We cannot have contact with influences that are degrading without being affected adversely, almost as though the degrading words and deeds become a part of us. On the other hand, if we regularly call upon God, pour out our soul in prayer, and yearn for genuine communion with Deity, we cannot help but be elevated and transformed by that association. The very powers of God, coming to us through his Holy Spirit, make us into men and women of purpose, of purity, and of power. In short, we pray in order to receive an infusion of power, to draw strength from an omnipotent Being.

> Oh, may my soul commune with thee
> And find thy holy peace;
> From worldly care and pain of fear,
> Please bring me sweet release.
>
> Oh, bless me when I worship thee
> To keep my heart in tune,
> That I may hear thy still, small voice,
> And, Lord, with thee commune.

Enfold me in thy quiet hour
And gently guide my mind
To seek thy will, to know thy ways,
And thy sweet Spirit find.

Lord, grant me thy abiding love
And make my turmoil cease.
Oh, may my soul commune with thee
*And find thy holy peace.*²

There are certain barriers to communion with the Infinite, things that get in the way and prevent us from enjoying the kind of closeness with our Heavenly Father that we could have. Let me suggest but a few.

Surely no roadblock could be more prevalent than distraction and preoccupation. Sometimes we don't pray well because our minds and hearts are focused on other things. We are too prone to think of prayer as something within the spiritual realm and of religion as just another department of life. Communion with the Infinite requires discipline, and discipline requires making priorities. Obviously we need to chase wickedness out of our lives if we are to draw close to God in prayer. But, in addition, when it is time to pray, we must put aside the things of the world, even good things, in order to engage the greatest good. We do not rush into the divine presence, any more than we would rush into the office of the president of the Church or the president of the United States. It is often helpful, before we begin to pray, to slow down, stop what we're doing, sit quietly, listen to inspiring music, read several verses of scripture, or ponder and reflect on things that matter most.

Another roadblock to an effective prayer life is duplicity, or trying to lead two lives. James explained that "a double minded man is unstable in all his ways" (James 1:8). Thus we would suppose that a person who is worldly throughout the day would have great difficulty praying intently at night. Elder Howard W. Hunter observed: "Henry Ward Beecher once said: 'It is not well for a man to pray cream and live skim milk.' . . . That was a century ago. There is now before us a danger that many may pray skim milk and live *that* not at all."[3] Just as our lives are only as good as our prayers, so our prayers are only as good as our lives. That is, the more faithful we become in keeping the Lord's commandments and putting first things first in our lives, the more we open the doors of communication with the heavens and the more comfortable we feel with holy things and holy beings.

Perhaps one common shortcoming is to say our prayers regularly but to do so without much thought, reflection, or devotion, except when we suppose that we really need God's help. Yet we know that we need his help every moment of every day of our lives. As King Benjamin pointed out to his people, God "is preserving you from day to day, by lending you breath, that ye may live and move and do according to your own will, and even supporting you from one moment to another" (Mosiah 2:21). Elder Hunter explained: "If prayer is only a spasmodic cry at the time of crisis, then it is utterly selfish, and we come to think of God as a repairman or a service agency to help us only in our emergencies. We should remember the Most High day and night—always—not only at times when all other assistance has failed and we desperately need help. If there is any element in human life on which we have a record of miraculous success and inestimable worth to the human soul, it is prayerful, reverential, devout communication with our Heavenly Father."[4] One practice that I have found particularly meaningful—especially when I find myself reciting words instead of communing with God—is to devote myself to a prayer in which I ask the Lord for absolutely nothing but instead express sincere gratitude for all my blessings. This kind of prayer pays remarkable dividends and settles the soul as few other things will.

Coach Vince Lombardi wisely remarked that fatigue makes cowards of us all. Fatigue also makes it extremely difficult to enjoy our prayers. Perhaps it is not always wise to make our prayers the last thing we do each day. It may be worthwhile occasionally to have prayer well before going to bed, while our mind and body are able to do more than utter a few well-worn and familiar phrases. There have been several times over the years when one of my children has talked me into watching a late movie with them, perhaps on a Friday night. Knowing that inevitably I would fall asleep, either on the floor or on the couch, more than once I have gone into my bedroom, closed the door, and had a meaningful prayer before going downstairs to watch the movie.

It is a marvelous thing—although perhaps we do not think about it very much—to be called upon to offer prayer in a public meeting. It is an honor to address the Almighty God, but it is a special honor to be asked to do so on behalf of a group of fellow believers. We damage ourselves spiritually and rob ourselves of a small but significant opportunity to grow when we decline such invitations to pray. Some refuse because they feel shy or afraid. They should take heart, for we are all in this together. No one of us has all of the answers, and no one of us has achieved such great spiritual heights that he or she is in a position to judge another's prayer, no matter how simple or halting it might be. Others may refuse to pray because they do not feel worthy to do so. With the exception of those who are under Church discipline and have thus been asked by priesthood leaders not to participate in public meetings, all are worthy to pray if called upon.

Nephi explained the source of an attitude that refuses to pray. "If ye would hearken unto the Spirit which teacheth a man to pray," he wrote, "ye would know that ye must pray; for the evil spirit teacheth not a man to pray, but teacheth him that he must not pray" (2 Nephi 32:8). The officers of the Church are charged to "visit the house of each member, and exhort them to pray vocally and in secret and attend to all family duties" (D&C 20:47; see also v. 51). Elsewhere the Savior instructs the Saints: "I command thee that thou shalt pray vocally as well as in thy heart; yea, before the world as well as in secret, in public as well as in private" (D&C 19:28; compare 23:6; 81:3).

There are some things we ought to keep in mind when we pray vocally. My father was fond of saying that we should pray for the occasion, meaning that we ought to consider why we are gathered together, what is needed most, and how we might best express those needs to our Father in Heaven. For one thing, public prayers, with perhaps the exception of dedicatory prayers, are and should be relatively short.

There may be occasions when it is necessary to take more time in prayer than usual, but such is rarely the case in public meetings. Shauna and I still remember attending a missionary farewell more than twenty-five years ago for a couple who had been called to serve a full-time mission. A number of people were called upon to speak—those were the days when sacrament meetings were an hour and a half long—but grandpa was not one of them. He was, however, asked to offer the opening prayer. I can still remember our two eldest children, who were just learning to bow their little heads and keep their eyes closed for more than a few seconds, glancing up with a puzzled look as the elderly gentleman spoke in great detail in his prayer of Christ, the different dimensions of the Atonement, and a variety of other doctrinal topics. The prayer, which lasted for seventeen minutes, seemed somewhat out of place. Our prayers are not sermons; they are not public discourses. They are addressed not to other Saints but to God. Elder Francis M. Lyman taught: "It is not necessary to offer very long and tedious prayers, either at opening or closing. It is not only not pleasing to the Lord for us to use excess of words, but also it is not pleasing to the Latter-day Saints. Two minutes will open any kind of meeting, and a half minute will close it."[5]

Two keys to meaningful prayer, including public prayer, are sincerity and simplicity. We have no one to impress, no one's judgment to fear. Our words are addressed to him who knows all things, including the desires of our hearts (D&C 6:16). It is thus wise to speak the words that we really feel. In Shakespeare's *Hamlet*, Claudius stopped praying because his heart was simply not in his prayers. He said, "My words fly up, my thoughts remain below; / Words without thoughts never to heaven go" (Act III, scene 3). The Prophet Joseph Smith taught in regard to prayer, "Be plain and simple, and ask for what you want, just like you would go to a neighbor and say, 'I want to borrow your horse to go to the mill.'"[6] As a part of his own prayer to God, Zenos exclaimed, "Yea, thou art merciful unto thy children when they cry unto thee, to be heard of thee and not of men, and thou wilt hear them" (Alma 33:8).

When we are called upon to pray, we should pray from our hearts with the dignity and respect due the God whom we are addressing. I am often pained as people hurry through a prayer as though it were a formality that needed to be dispensed with as quickly and painlessly as possible. That is particularly true for the end of the prayer. We should close our prayers with the dignity and transcendent respect that we ought to have for the name of him who bought us with his blood, the Savior of all mankind. Sometimes people are so eager to be finished with the prayer that they race through the name of Jesus Christ as though they were sprinting toward a finish line. That cannot be pleasing to his Father, who is also our Father. If we pray sincerely, from our hearts, speaking our words soberly and distinctly—especially the concluding words, "in the name of Jesus Christ"—we will begin to feel a power and a sacred influence in our lives that attests that the Lord hears us and is pleased with us.

One thing most needed in our prayer lives is consistency and regularity. Some people find it helpful to pray in the same place. One man I know set aside a special room in his home, a place which over the years came to be like his personal sacred grove. It seemed when he entered that room that he felt a hallowed presence. In fact, because some of the most profound insights and some of the sweetest feelings and impressions came to him in that room, it represented almost a holy of holies within his templed home.

Nearly forty years ago another man taught me something that changed my life. He said simply, "When you get out of bed in the morning, never let your feet touch the floor first. Always let your knees touch first." I recommend that bit of practical wisdom, especially if you find it difficult to have a regular, meaningful morning prayer. I have been surprised at how many people who would never consider going to bed without praying in the evening have not developed a consistent pattern of prayer in the mornings.

In practical terms, I have thought that there are very few harmful or hazardous things that could happen to me between the time I lay my head on the pillow at night and the time I get up, but there are many challenges and temptations and decisions I must face throughout the day, and I need all the help I can get. Evening prayers are extremely important, and morning prayers are vital.

Two of my colleagues at Brigham Young University, Brent Top and Bruce Chadwick, have told me that their studies of morality and faithfulness in Latter-day Saint youth throughout the Church reveal that LDS young people who remained steadfast, solid, and straight in the midst of serious temptation were those whose parents had helped them to internalize the gospel, to make personal scripture study and especially personal prayer high priorities in their lives. The following are some comments from active young Latter-day Saints who made it through challenges without losing their way, at least so far:

"I am so blessed now because my parents encouraged me to pray and read the scriptures on my own."

"My dad always reminds me, 'Say your prayers.' This reminds me that it is not enough to have family prayer. I must pray on my own."

"My parents taught me how important personal revelation is and how I could find answers in the scriptures and receive answers to my prayers."

"It was my parents' example that had the most effect on me. . . . They would give thoughts and advice, but they left it up to me. But they would always counsel me to turn to the Lord and find out his will. In doing this it helped me to start to have spiritual experiences in my own life."[7]

These comments affirm the promise of President Ezra Taft

Benson, who said to the youth, "If you will earnestly seek guidance from your Heavenly Father, morning and evening, you will be given the strength to shun any temptation."[8] We all know that such a promise applies equally to the rest of us.

Awake, ye Saints of God, awake!
Call on the Lord in mighty prayer
That he will Zion's bondage break
And bring to naught the tempter's snare.

Tho Zion's foes have counseled deep,
Although they bind with fetters strong,
The God of Jacob does not sleep;
His vengeance will not slumber long.

With constant faith and fervent prayer,
With deep humility of soul,
With steadfast mind and heart, prepare
To see th' eternal purpose roll.

Awake to righteousness; be one,
Or, saith the Lord, "Ye are not mine!"
Yea, like the Father and the Son,
Let all the Saints in union join.[9]

There are prayers, and then there are prayers. Sometimes we need to pray with a light spirit and without heavy and deep need weighing upon us. At other times, we long for the kind of spiritual contact and association that demand our most strenuous and disciplined efforts. Jacob of old wrestled with an angel until the breaking of day and thus obtained a blessing from God (Genesis 32:24–32). Hungering and thirsting after righteousness, Enos wrestled with the Lord in prayer all day and into the night, until the holy voice declared that his sins were forgiven (Enos 1:1–8). Our Lord and Savior came to know something about prayer that he could not have known before his entrance into mortality. In the Garden of Gethsemane, the Savior began to feel the loss of his Father's sustaining Spirit. "And being in an agony," Luke records, "he prayed more earnestly" (Luke 22:44). In writing of this singular occasion, Elder Bruce R. McConkie observed: "Now here is a marvelous thing. Note it well. The Son of God 'prayed more earnestly'! He who did all things well, whose every word was right, whose every emphasis was proper; he to whom the Father gave his Spirit without measure; he who was the only perfect being ever to walk the dusty paths of planet earth—the Son of God 'prayed more earnestly,' teaching us, his brethren [and sisters], that all prayers, his included, are not alike, and that a greater need calls forth more earnest and faith-filled pleadings before the throne of him to whom the prayers of the saints are a sweet savor."[10]

Indeed, some thorns in the flesh call forth prayers of great intensity (2 Corinthians 12:7–10), supplications and pleadings that are certainly out of the ordinary. Such vexations of the soul are not typical, not part of our daily prayer life. Just as it would be a mistake to suppose that Jacob or Enos wrestled with God in prayer every day, so you and I are not expected to involve ourselves with the same tenacity, to be involved in the same bending of the soul on a regular basis. But now and then, in the eternal scheme of things, we must pass through the fire to come through life purified and refined and thus prepared to dwell one day in everlasting burnings with God and Christ and other holy beings.

If we are willing to move beyond a casual relationship with God, willing to spend the time and exert the energy necessary to make of our prayer life something more than it is now, then great things await us. For one thing, in time and with experience, our prayers can become more than petitions, as important as it is to petition the Lord. Our prayers can become instructive, the means whereby God can reveal great and important things to us. The apostle Paul taught us that "the Spirit also helpeth our infirmities: for we know not what we should pray for as we ought: but the Spirit itself maketh intercession for us with [striving] which cannot be [expressed]" (Romans 8:26).[11] That is to say, if we are quiet and attentive, the Spirit of the Lord can, on some occasions, lead us to pray for things that were not on our personal agenda, things deep down, things that pertain more to our eternal needs than our temporal wants. At such times we find our words reaching beyond our thoughts, praying for people and circumstances and eventualities that surprise us.

"God sees things as they really are," Elder Neal A. Maxwell wrote, "and as they will become. We don't! In order to tap that precious perspective during our prayers, we must rely upon the promptings of the Holy Ghost. With access to that kind of knowledge, we would then pray for what we and others should have—*really* have. With the Spirit prompting us, we will not pray 'amiss.'

"With access to the Spirit, our circles of concern will expand. The mighty prayer of Enos began with understandable self-concern, moved outward to family, then to his enemies, and then outward to future generations."[12]

We kneel before God to show our reverence toward him and where possible speak our prayers aloud, but many times in the day we are not able to kneel or give voice to our yearnings or our feelings. So it is that we have the commission to "pray always," to keep a prayer in our hearts, to speak to the Almighty in our mind. We pray for his direction and his strength in school, in our work, in our studies, in our athletic endeavors, and in counseling with troubled friends or confused loved ones. Amulek invites us to "cry unto him for mercy; for he is mighty to save. Yea, humble yourselves, and continue in prayer unto him. Cry unto him when ye are in your fields, yea, over all your flocks. Cry unto him in your houses, yea, over all your household, both morning, mid-day, and evening. Yea, cry unto him against the power of your enemies. Yea, cry unto him against the devil, who is an enemy to all righteousness. Cry unto him over the crops of your fields, that ye may prosper in them. Cry over the flocks of your fields, that they may increase. But this is not all; ye must pour out your souls in your closets, and your secret places, and in your wilderness. Yea, and when you do not cry unto the Lord, let your hearts be full, drawn out in prayer unto him continually for your welfare, and also for the welfare of those who are around you" (Alma 34:18–27).

Alma also implored, "Cry unto God for all thy support; yea, let all thy doings be unto the Lord, and whithersoever thou goest let it be in the Lord; yea, let all thy thoughts be directed unto the Lord; yea, let the affections of thy heart be placed upon the Lord forever. Counsel with the Lord in all thy doings, and he will direct thee for good; yea, when thou liest down at night lie down unto the Lord, that he may watch over you in your sleep; and when thou risest in the morning let thy heart be full of thanks unto God; and if ye do these things, ye shall be lifted up at the last day" (Alma 37:36–37).

As President Boyd K. Packer pointed out some years ago, the moral pollution index in our society is rising.[13] Evil is on the loose. "Satan is abroad in the land" (D&C 52:14); it is truly the day of his power. We cannot resist the incessant pull of immorality nor escape the desensitization that follows naturally from larger doses of harshness, crudeness, and violence without the infusion of spiritual power that comes through communion with the Infinite. No one of us in invulnerable to satanic influences. No one of us is strong enough to confront the enemy alone.

I know that prayer makes available that balm of Gilead that comes to us from God in heaven through his Holy Spirit. Peace and perspective come to us as we come unto him. I know that God our Father lives, that he knows us and hears our prayers. When we pray, we are speaking not to a force in the universe but to the Father of our spirits. I know that we can refine and purify our lives through a greater attention to the regularity, intensity, and overall quality of our prayers. That we will more consistently pour out our souls in prayer as individuals and as families that the Lord may pour out upon us a blessing hitherto unknown, is the earnest desire of my heart.

NOTES

1. McKay, *True to the Faith*, 244–45.
2. *Hymns*, no. 123.
3. Hunter, Conference Report, October 1977, 79; italics in original.
4. Hunter, Conference Report, October 1977, 79.
5. Lyman, address delivered at MIA Conference, 5 June 1892; reprinted in *Improvement Era*, April 1947, 245.
6. As cited in Andrus and Andrus, *They Knew the Prophet*, 100.
7. Top and Chadwick, *Rearing Righteous Teens*, 89.
8. Benson, Conference Report, October 1977, 46.
9. *Hymns*, no. 17.
10. McConkie, "Why the Lord Ordained Prayer," in *Prayer*, 8.
11. Compare *Teachings of the Prophet Joseph Smith*, 278; 3 Nephi 19:24; D&C 46:30; 50:29–30; 63:65.
12. Maxwell, "What Should We Pray For?" in *Prayer*, 45; italics in original.
13. Packer, Conference Report, April 1992, 91.

CHAPTER 10

DON'T DESPAIR

I HAVE LEARNED THAT IF SATAN cannot get us to break the Word of Wisdom or the law of chastity, to speak evil of the Lord's anointed, or in general bristle at the demands of discipleship, he will try to discourage us. He will throw things into our path over which we stumble and fall and bruise ourselves. And, to be sure, there are a myriad of things about which we can get discouraged. I am inclined to believe that we in the early stages of the twenty-first century are more susceptible to stress and distress, to despondency and discouragement than our forebears were. Certainly life is more complex, the demands on our time are more intense, and the temptations of the devil are more sophisticated. At the same time, it seems to me that there is a mind-set, characteristic of our day, that leaves us open to despair.

That mind-set is one in which we assume, given all the pleasures and luxuries of our day and age, that all should be well with us at all times, that we should be perpetually happy. Many of us have bought into and imbibed the jargon and the philosophy of our pop psychology world. People throughout the world—and some are Latter-day Saints—spend an unbelievable amount of time and an inordinate amount of money trying to "find themselves," to achieve the measure of personal fulfillment that life is supposed to guarantee all participants. The truth is, life can be tough. We are not guaranteed a stress-free existence, nor did the Lord promise us a mortal life void of challenge and difficulty. Elder Boyd K. Packer stated: "We live in a day when the adversary stresses on every hand the philosophy of instant gratification. We seem to demand *instant* everything, including instant solutions to our problems.

"We are indoctrinated that somehow we should always be instantly emotionally comfortable. When that is not so, some become anxious—and all too frequently seek relief from counseling, from analysis, and even from medication.

"It was meant to be that life would be a challenge. To suffer some anxiety, some depression, some disappointment, even some failure is normal.

"Teach our members that if they have a good, miserable day once in a while, or several in a row, to stand steady and face them. Things will straighten out.

"There is great purpose in our struggle in life."[1]

Simply stated, we are now living in a fallen world, one in which things break down, decay, atrophy, and die. We are living in a mortal existence. This is not act 3 of the play but act 2. "Happily ever after" refers not to this world but to the next. There is much in the world that is glorious and beautiful and uplifting and inspiring; many of the relationships we establish are elevating and enriching—they bring the deepest of joys into our lives. But we receive our joys alongside our sorrows. Both elements of the equation come with the earth. We knew that before we came here.

C. S. Lewis pointed out that too often human beings struggle with the philosophical question of evil and suffering in the world—that is, we question how an all-wise, all-loving, and all-powerful Deity could allow horrible things to happen to his children—because of what we think of God and what we suppose his object for us is. "By the goodness of God we mean nowadays almost exclusively His lovingness; and in this way we may be right. And by Love, in this context, most of us mean kindness—the desire to see others than the self happy; not happy in this way or in that, but just happy. What would really satisfy us would be a God who said of anything we happened to like doing, 'What does it matter so long as they are contented?' We want, in fact, not so much a Father in Heaven as a grandfather—a senile benevolence who, as they say, 'liked to see young people enjoying themselves,' and whose plan for the universe was simply that it might be truly said at the end of each day, 'a good time was had by all.'" Lewis went on to say that God has paid us the "intolerable compliment" of loving us, "in the deepest, most tragic, most inexorable sense. We are," he continued, "not metaphorically but in very truth, a Divine work of art, something that God is making, and therefore something with which He will not be satisfied until it has a certain character." Thus it is perfectly "natural for us to wish that God had designed for us a less glorious and less arduous destiny; but then we are wishing not for more love but for less."[2]

"For whom the Lord loveth he chasteneth, and scourgeth every son whom he receiveth. . . . Now no chastening for the present seemeth to be joyous, but grievous: nevertheless afterward it yieldeth the peaceable fruit of righteousness unto them which are exercised [trained, disciplined] thereby" (Hebrews 12:6, 11). James, the brother of Jesus, therefore instructed us to "count it all joy when ye fall into many afflictions; knowing this, that the trying of your faith worketh patience. But let patience have her perfect work, that ye may be perfect and entire, wanting nothing" (JST James 1:2–4).

There are great lessons to be learned from life's struggles, lessons that can perhaps be acquired in no other way. Many of our afflictions we bring upon ourselves through our own impatience, shortsightedness, or sins. There are even lessons to be learned from our sins—not the least of which is motivation to avoid in the future the pain associated with our misdeeds—but those are lessons I am persuaded the Lord can bring into our lives without our sinning. A man called as a bishop, for example, need not be troubled about the fact that he has lived a faithful life and thus may not be able to feel what the transgressor feels. The Great Physician, he who descended below all things during the awful hours of atonement (D&C 88:6; 122:8), is able, through his Holy Spirit, to reveal to his ordained servants what they need to know and feel in order to lead the wandering sheep back into the fold.

When I was young, I had a teacher who repeatedly said, "Now you folks know that I am not perfect and that I haven't lived a perfect life. I've done this and this and this, but I want you to know that I repented and am a better man because of it." I didn't believe that when I heard it as a youth, and I don't believe it now. We do not need to sin in order to appreciate the value of righteousness. We do not need to stray in order to appreciate the safety and security of the strait and narrow path. "The idea that one is better off after one has sinned and repented is a devilish lie of the adversary," Elder Dallin H. Oaks explained. "Does anyone here think that it is better to learn firsthand that a certain blow will break a bone or a certain mixture of chemicals will explode and sear off our skin? . . . I believe we all can see that it is better to heed the warnings of wise persons who know the effects on our bodies of certain traumas.

"Just as we can benefit from someone else's experience in matters such as these, we can also benefit from the warnings contained in the commandments of God. We don't have to have personal experience with the effects of serious transgressions to know that they are destructive of our eternal welfare."[3] It is far better to prepare and prevent than it is to repair and repent.

But there are lessons that come to us from God through challenges and distresses and setbacks and failures. Pain performs a purifying work, a divine work that can transform the soul of the distressed one, if he or she approaches the difficulty with the proper attitude. It is not uncommon for members of the Church who have lost a loved one, or who face the prospects of a terminal disease, or whose fortunes have been dramatically reversed, to ask, Why? Why would God do this to me? Why is this happening? These are, of course, "natural" reactions to trauma, especially when each us would be perfectly content to remain perfectly content! But that's not why we are here.

On more than one occasion I have suggested to sufferers, as kindly and lovingly as I could, that Why is this happening? is not the proper question. We know the answer. It is happening because we are mortal, because painful things happen in a mortal world. No one of us is required by God to enjoy suffering or to anticipate with delight the next trial, but it makes little sense for us to come to earth to be proven and then to ask why we are being proven. The Father is the Husbandman, the Vinedresser. The Savior is the Vine, and we are the branches. The Vinedresser chooses the manner in which he will purge the branches. Why? "Every branch that beareth fruit," the Master stated, "he [the Father] purgeth it, that it may bring forth more fruit" (John 15:2).

Viktor Frankl has written that "we who lived in concentration camps can remember the men who walked through the huts comforting others, giving away their last piece of bread. They may have been few in number, but they offer sufficient proof that everything can be taken from a man but one thing: the last of . . . human freedoms—to choose one's attitude in any given set of circumstances, [and] to choose one's own way [of life]."[4] As difficult as it is to acknowledge this truth, we must be willing to be "broken" if we really expect to gain that broken heart and contrite spirit about which the scriptures speak (Psalm 51:17; 3 Nephi 9:20; D&C 59:8). Inasmuch as our will is the only thing that we can, in the long run, really consecrate to God, the Lord needs to know of our willingness to be broken by him—that is, he needs to know to what degree we are willing to submit, to surrender, to yield our hearts unto him.

"What happens in the breaking of a horse?" someone asked. "Contrary to what many people believe, the horse's spirit isn't broken. A well-broken horse remains strong, eager, quick-witted, and aware, and he loves to gallop when given free rein. Rather, it is the horse's independence that is broken. The breaking of a horse results in the horse giving instant obedience to its rider.

"When a child of God is broken, God does not destroy his or her spirit. We don't lose our zest for living when we come to Christ. We don't lose the force of our personality. Rather, we lose our independence. Our will is brought into submission to the will of the Father so that we can give instant obedience to the one whom we call Savior and Lord. . . .

"We can choose to respond to brokenness with anger, bitterness, and hate. We can rail against our circumstances. We can strike out against those whom we believe have caused us pain. Those options are available to us because we have free will.

"The way to blessing, however, lies in turning to God to heal us and make us whole. We decide whether we will yield to him and trust him."[5] Indeed, if we approach them properly, our trials can teach and sanctify us, can assist us to know the fellowship of Christ's suffering (Philippians 3:10). Francis Webster, one of those who suffered unspeakable pain as a member of the Martin Handcart Company, said, "Every one of us came through with the absolute knowledge that God lives, for we became acquainted with him in our extremities."[6]

At a very difficult time for my wife, Shauna, and me—when we watched helplessly as loved ones chose painful and unproductive paths—we found ourselves, early in the process of dealing with the pain, at a crossroads. We sensed at that early juncture that our attitude toward what we were experiencing was essential. To be honest, both of us went through periods of weeks and months in which our days were filled with self-doubt, with personal recrimination, with loads of questions about what we had done wrong over the years. But as we prayed with intensity, read the scriptures with new and searching eyes, and spent time regularly in the holy temple, there began to distill upon us the quiet but powerful realization that we could determine how we would deal with our dilemma. Would we allow our problems to strangle our marriage and family? Would we permit these difficulties to drive us into seclusion? Would we yield to doubt and cynicism, given that we had tried so hard through the years to do what we were asked? I will be forever grateful that the two of us sensed that we must face that trial together and that the one thing we could not afford was for it to drive the two of us apart. Further, after a time of being wrung out emotionally and spiritually, we both sensed that the Lord was our only hope for peace, our only means of extricating ourselves from dysfunctional living. It was then that our prayers and our yearnings began to change. It was then that we found ourselves shorn of self-concern and naked in our ineptitude; it was then that we acknowledged our nothingness and drew upon the strength and lifting power of our Divine Redeemer. We were still concerned, and we kept trying, but we were "trying in a new way, a less worried way."[7]

As Elder Packer suggested, we should not be unnerved by trials and challenges and even a bad day once in a while. And there are certainly times when a third party, be it a priesthood leader, parent, dear friend, or even a professional counselor, can assist us to put things in place or in proper perspective. It may even be necessary in some instances for an individual to have medication prescribed by a competent physician. But we must never, ever, minimize the healing effect the Master can have in our lives, the calming and reassuring and healing balm that he can be to us, no matter the depth of our despair or the seriousness of our situation.

"Whatever Jesus lays his hands upon lives," Elder Howard W. Hunter testified. "If Jesus lays his hands upon a marriage, it lives. If he is allowed to lay his hands upon the family, it lives."[8] The touch of the Master's hand is life and light and love. It

calms. It soothes. It sanctifies. It empowers. It transcends anything earthly. Truly, the greatest miracles we see today, declared
President Harold B. Lee, "are not necessarily the healing of sick
bodies, but the greatest miracles [we] see today are the healing
of sick souls, those who are sick in soul and spirit and are
downhearted and distraught."[9] These are they who can joy-
ously proclaim, like Andrew, Simon Peter's brother, "We have
found the Messias" (John 1:41).

Sometimes we get down on ourselves unnecessarily. We
look at our lives and find that we are not yet where we thought
we would be at this point. What we fail to realize is just how
far we have come; we forget to look back at the valley below
and realize how far up the mountain of spirituality we have
climbed. There is nothing wrong with wanting to improve,
leave the plateau, and move onward and upward. But we must
not allow our zeal for rapid progress and growth to blind us to
whatever past progress we have made. Divine discontent must
be balanced with feelings of accomplishment.

Another principle to consider in dealing with discouragement is that as we lose ourselves in service to others, we find
ourselves in the truest sense. During the time my wife and I
were struggling with family matters, I was serving as bishop
and she was for a while serving as Relief Society president. Both
of us found, again and again, that as we focused away from
ourselves and our problems, as we put away our own troubles
and gave ourselves to others, the Lord lifted our burdens and
soothed our aching souls. President Lorenzo Snow stated:
"When you find yourselves a little gloomy, look around you
and find somebody that is in a worse plight than yourself; go
to him and find out what the trouble is, then try to remove it
with the wisdom which the Lord bestows upon you; and the

first thing you know, your gloom is gone, you feel light, the Spirit of the Lord is upon you, and everything seems illuminated."[10]

I do not wish to seem to minimize in any way the tremendous challenges that many of our people face. They are real and sobering. I am very much aware that many have been subjected to much pain and distress in their lives, to abuse, to neglect, to the agonies of wanting to live a normal life and to feel normal feelings but who seem unable to do so. I would say, first of all, that each of us, whoever we are, wrestles with something. Perhaps it's something like weight or height or complexion or baldness or I.Q. Perhaps it's something that passes in time, like a phase. Perhaps it's the torture of watching helplessly as loved ones choose unwisely and thereby close doors of opportunity for themselves and foreclose future privileges. Perhaps it's those occasions when someone we love does despite to our tender trust and deals a blow that strikes at the center of all we hold dear and all we value about ourselves.

I know that the day is coming when all the wrongs, the awful wrongs of this life, will be righted, when the God of justice will attend to all evil. Things that are beyond our power to control will be corrected, either here or hereafter. Many of us may come to enjoy the lifting, liberating powers of the Atonement in this life, and our losses may be made up before we pass from this sphere of existence. Perhaps some of us will wrestle all our days with our traumas and our trials, for he who orchestrates the events of our lives will surely fix the time of our release. I have a conviction that when a person passes through the veil of death, all the impediments and challenges and crosses that were beyond his or her power to control— abuse, neglect, immoral environment, weighty traditions, and so forth—will be torn away like a film and perfect peace will prevail in our hearts. "Some frustrations," Elder Boyd K. Packer taught, "we must endure without really solving the problem. Some things that ought to be put in order are not put in order because we cannot control them. Things we cannot solve, we must survive."[11]

In some cases our Lord and Master seems to ask of us the impossible—to forgive those who have hurt us so dreadfully. As Bruce and Marie Hafen have observed, "It seems fair to ask why the victims of abuse should be required to do *anything* to deserve the Lord's vast healing powers in such a case. Because abuse victims suffer so many of the same symptoms of guilt and estrangement from God as do willful transgressors, the irony that they should need to forgive those who have wronged them is almost overpowering.

"Still, there lurks between the lines of the scriptures on forgiveness a message of transcendent meaning—not only about abuse victims but about all of us, and about all of the Atonement." The Hafens continue: "What are we doing when we are willing to absorb a terrible trauma of the spirit, caused not by our own doing but by one who claimed to love us—and we absorb the trauma even to help the sinner? That picture somehow has a familiar look—we've seen all this before. Of course, because this picture depicts the sacrifice of Jesus Christ: he took upon himself undeserved and unbearable burdens, heaped upon him by people who often said, and often believed, that they loved him. And he assumed that load not for any need of his, but only to help them.

"So to forgive—not just for abuse victims, but for each of us—is to be a Christ figure, a transitional point in the war between good and evil, stopping the current of evil by absorbing it in every pore, thereby protecting the innocent next generation and helping to enable the repentance and healing of those whose failures sent the jolts into our own systems."[12]

And so we hold on, we press on, we move ahead, even though the road is not necessarily straight and the path is not necessarily cleared. As President Ezra Taft Benson declared: "There are times when you simply have to righteously hang on and outlast the devil until his depressive spirit leaves you. . . . To press on in noble endeavors, even while surrounded by a cloud of depression, will eventually bring you out on top into the sunshine. Even our master Jesus the Christ, while facing that supreme test of being temporarily left alone by our Father during the crucifixion, continued performing his labors for the children of men, and then shortly thereafter he was glorified and received a fullness of joy. While you are going through your trial, you can recall your past victories and count the blessings that you do have with a sure hope of greater ones to follow if you are faithful. And you can have that certain knowledge that in due time God will wipe away all tears and that 'eye hath not seen, nor ear heard, neither have entered into the heart of man, the things which God hath prepared for them that love him.' (1 Corinthians 2:9.)."[13]

NOTES

1. Packer, Conference Report, April 1978, 139–40; italics in original.
2. Lewis, *Problem of Pain*, 35–36, 38.
3. Oaks, "Sin and Suffering," 151.
4. Frankl, *Man's Search for Meaning*, 86.
5. Stanley, *Blessings of Brokenness*, 47–48, 53.
6. Cited in Faust, *Finding Light in a Dark World*, 55.
7. Lewis, *Mere Christianity*, 131.
8. Hunter, Conference Report, October 1979, 93.
9. Lee, Conference Report, April 1973, 178.

10. Snow, Conference Report, April 1899, 2–3.

11. Packer, Conference Report, October 1987, 20.

12. Hafen and Hafen, *Belonging Heart,* 122–23.

13. Benson, Conference Report, October 1974, 93.

CHAPTER 11

SETTLED AND ESTABLISHED

A SIGN OF OUR SPIRITUAL GROWTH is steadiness, our capacity to navigate the strait and narrow path in a stable and fairly consistent manner, to work with zeal but patient maturity, to stay in the mainstream of the Church. God does not expect us to work ourselves into spiritual, emotional, or physical exhaustion, nor does he desire that the members of the true Church be truer than true. There is no virtue in excess, even in gospel excess. In fact, as members of the Church exceed the bounds of propriety and go beyond the established mark, they open themselves to deception and ultimately to destruction. Imbalance leads to instability. If Satan cannot entice us to sins of commission, it just may be that he will cause our strength—our zeal for goodness and righteousness—to become our weakness. He will encourage excess, for surely any virtue, when taken to the extreme, may become a vice.

Persons who determine upon a course that will take them beyond the expected, above the required, inevitably begin to expect the same of others. It becomes a "religious" principle,

125

one to which persons are proselyted. The overzealous tend to judge others by their own standard. I have known persons who were so completely committed to family history and temple work that they occasionally badgered and criticized others who might not have been in a position to do as much as they themselves were doing. Obviously such work is a vital part of our ministry as Latter-day Saints; we neglect it at the peril of our eternal salvation. I also know, as Elder Dallin H. Oaks has pointed out, that there is a time and a season for all things, that individuals' specific contributions to the kingdom are and must be private consecrations between the individuals and God. That is why the leaders of the Church have discouraged quotas and goals for temple work. "Our efforts to promote temple and family history work," Elder Oaks has noted, "should be such as to accomplish the work of the Lord, not to impose guilt on his children. Members of this church have many individual circumstances—age, health, education, place of residence, family responsibilities, financial circumstances, accessibility to sources for individual or library research, and many others. If we encourage members in this work without taking these individual circumstances into account, we may do more to impose guilt than to further the work. . . .

"There are many different things our members can do to help in the redeeming of the dead, in temple and family history work. Some involve callings. . . . All are expressions of devotion and discipleship. All present opportunities for sacrifice and service."[1]

We could take a simple observance, such as fasting or praying, and soon find that the slightest amount of extra zeal in applying such principles, which have been given for the blessing and benefit of mankind, contributes to error. "Gospel hobbies," the tendency to take a good thing and run it into the ground, are some of the evils of excess, even in noble and worthwhile causes. Gospel hobbies lead to imbalance. To instability. To distraction. To misperception. They are dangerous and should be avoided as we would any other sin. President Joseph F. Smith said: "We frequently look about us and see people who incline to extremes, who are fanatical. We may be sure that this class of people do not understand the gospel. They have forgotten, if they ever knew, that it is very unwise to take a fragment of truth and treat it as if it were the whole thing."[2] To ride a gospel hobby is to participate in fanaticism and perpetuate it. Harsh words, but true ones. On another occasion President Smith taught: "Brethren and sisters, don't have hobbies. Hobbies are dangerous in the Church of Christ. They are dangerous because they give undue prominence to certain principles or ideas to the detriment and dwarfing of others just as important, just as binding, just as saving as the favored doctrines or commandments.

"Hobbies give to those who encourage them a false aspect of the gospel of the Redeemer; they distort and place out of harmony its principles and teachings. The point of view is unnatural. Every principle and practice revealed from God is essential to man's salvation, and to place any one of them unduly in front, hiding and dimming all others is unwise and dangerous; it jeopardizes our salvation, for it darkens our minds and beclouds our understandings. . . .

"We have noticed this difficulty: that Saints with hobbies are prone to judge and condemn their brethren and sisters who are not so zealous in the one particular direction of their pet theory as they are. . . .

"There is another phase of this difficulty—the man with a

hobby is apt to assume an 'I am holier than thou' position, to feel puffed up and conceited, and to look with distrust, if with no severer feeling, on his brethren and sisters who do not so perfectly live that one particular law."[3]

In other words, an emphasis upon excellence in gospel living as manifest in gospel hobbies can result in pride, the father of all other sins. President Harold B. Lee explained that at times "people who pride themselves on their strict observance of the rules and ordinances and ceremonies of the Church are led astray by false spirits, who exercise an influence so imitative of that which proceeds from a Divine source that even these persons, who think they are 'the very elect,' find it difficult to discern the essential difference."[4] True excellence in gospel living—compliance with the established laws and ordinances in a quiet and patient manner—results in humility, greater reliance upon God, and a broadening love and acceptance of one's fellowman. There is a principle here: what we are doing in the name of goodness ought to bring us closer to those we love and serve, ought to turn our heart toward people rather than causing us to turn up our noses in judgmental scorn and rejection. The greatest man to walk the earth, the only fully perfect human being, looked with tenderness and compassion upon those whose ways and actions were less than perfect.

Elder Bruce R. McConkie similarly wrote: "It is . . . my experience that people who ride gospel hobbies, who try to qualify themselves as experts in some specialized field, who try to make the whole plan of salvation revolve around some field of particular interest to them—it is my experience that such persons are usually spiritually immature and spiritually unstable. This includes those who devote themselves—as though by divine appointment—to setting forth the signs of the times; or, to expounding about the Second Coming; or, to a faddist inter-pretation of the Word of Wisdom; or, to a twisted emphasis on temple work or any other doctrine or practice. The Jews of Jesus' day made themselves hobbiests and extremists in the field of Sabbath observance, and it colored and blackened their whole way of worship. We would do well to have a sane, rounded, and balanced approach to the whole gospel and all of its doctrines."[5]

Not unrelated to excessive zeal is the tendency by some to attempt to force spiritual things. What would we think of a father who said to his fourteen-year-old son: "Larry, if you really love me, you will be tall. I have been short all my life. I love basketball and have always wanted to be a star forward on a successful team, but it's never worked out. If you love me, if you have any respect for me as your father, you will grow to be six foot eight." Such a request would be cruel and unkind, especially given that Larry has little control over how tall he will be. He can eat the right foods, train and work out, and do everything within his power to become big and strong, but he cannot control how tall he will be.

In a way, it's just the same with spiritual growth. We can-not program it. We cannot specify and delineate and produce. We cannot prepare formulae and plans that will result in spe-cific spiritual phenomena. We cannot say with certitude that if individuals do X and Y and Z that a dream or vision will be forthcoming, or that if they do A or B or C consistently, they will be able to prophesy or speak in tongues. We can prepare the soil—provide a setting for development—but that is all. We must exercise patience and trust in the Lord and his purposes.

I knew one man who claimed that he would be perfect by the age of thirty. He set out on a deliberate program, organized his goals according to a ten-year, five-year, one-year, monthly, weekly, and daily plan. He pushed and pulled and stretched and reached spiritually as much as any person I have known. But he was not perfect at age thirty. Spiritual things cannot be forced. I am acquainted with a woman who announced to several of her friends that she would make her calling and election sure by the time she was fifty years old. She has been faithful in the Church. She has long since passed the age of fifty and is greatly discouraged because the goal of her existence, so far as she knows, has not been realized.

Spiritual things cannot be forced. Endless prayers, lengthy scripture vigils, excessive fasting—all of these, though at first well-intended, may come to be more a curse than a blessing. Gospel growth must come slowly, steadily, gradually. Elder Boyd K. Packer has warned: "Such words as *compel, coerce, constrain, pressure, demand* do not describe our privileges with the Spirit.

"You can no more force the Spirit to respond than you can force a bean to sprout, or an egg to hatch before its time. You can create a climate to foster growth; you can nourish, and protect; but you cannot force or compel: You must await the growth.

"Do not be impatient to gain great spiritual knowledge. Let it grow, help it grow; but do not force it, or you will open the way to be misled."[6]

Like the small oil lamps of the Middle East, which require a careful and methodical effort to fill, so in our own lives we need to build our reservoirs of faith and spiritual experience gradually and consistently. Consistent gospel growth—that is the way. A colleague of mine drew my attention to these words of President Spencer W. Kimball: "The foolish [virgins] asked the others to share their oil, but spiritual preparedness cannot be shared in an instant. . . . This was not selfishness or unkindness. The kind of oil that is needed to illuminate the way and light up the darkness is not shareable. . . . In our lives the oil of preparedness is accumulated drop by drop in righteous living."[7]

Finally, in our eagerness to prepare and do all that is required, we must be careful that our personal expectations, though rigorous, are realistic. Zion of old became a society of the pure in heart "in process of time" (Moses 7:21), and, with few exceptions, members of the Church become holy in similar fashion. Except for a limited number of cases so miraculous they are written up in scripture, being born again is a process; we are born again gradually, from one level of spiritual grace to a higher. Almost always people are sanctified—made clean and holy and pure through the blood of Christ by the medium of the Holy Ghost—in gradual, line-upon-line fashion. Ultimate perfection and salvation are processes.

The scriptures set forth certain principles which, if we are sensitive to their implications, will keep us on course and thus assist us in our quest for holiness. In his response to Satan's temptation to use divine powers for personal gain, the Savior answered: "It is written, Man shall not live by bread alone, but by every word that proceedeth out of the mouth of God" (Matthew 4:4; compare D&C 84:44). *Every* word. Not every other word, not those words that are most acceptable and pleasing, not those words that support my own peculiar predispositions. Every word. Members of the Church would seldom become embroiled in doctrinal disputes, controversial dialogues, or gospel hobbies if they truly sought to live by every word that has come from the Lord, the scriptures, and the servants of God. To live by every word of God also implies the need to read and study widely, to seek for at least as much breadth in our gospel scholarship as we have depth, to seek to have the big picture. It has been wisely said that the greatest commentary on the scriptures is the scriptures themselves.

In preaching to his American Hebrews, the resurrected Lord delivered the doctrine of Christ—the need for all men and women to have faith, repent, be reborn, and to endure faithfully to the end. He then declared: "Verily, verily, I say unto you, that this is my doctrine, and whoso buildeth upon this buildeth upon my rock, and the gates of hell shall not prevail against them. And whoso shall declare more or less than this, and establish it for my doctrine, the same cometh of evil, and is not built upon my rock; but he buildeth upon a sandy foundation, and the gates of hell stand open to receive such when the floods come and the winds beat upon them" (3 Nephi 11:39–40).

In a modern revelation, the Lord spoke of bringing forth the Book of Mormon, another testament of Jesus Christ, in order that he might establish his gospel and alleviate contention and disputation. "Behold, this is my doctrine—whosoever repenteth and cometh unto me, the same is my church. Whosoever declareth more or less than this, the same is not of me, but is against me; therefore he is not of my church" (D&C 10:67–68). We need to live the gospel in such a way that we seek neither to add to nor take away from that which comes by and through the appointed channels of revelation for the Church.

Not unrelated is the indictment sounded by Jacob against the ancient Jews. "The Jews were a stiffnecked people," he stated, "and they despised the words of plainness, and killed the prophets, and sought for things that they could not understand. Wherefore, because of their blindness, which blindness came by looking beyond the mark, they must needs fall; for God hath taken away his plainness from them, and delivered unto them many things which they cannot understand, because they desired it. And because they desired it God hath done it, that they may stumble" (Jacob 4:14). What a fascinating situation! A people despised, or perhaps spurned or little appreciated, the words of plainness. They sought for things they could not understand, perhaps meaning that they pushed themselves beyond what had been revealed and thus beyond what men and women could appropriately grasp. They became blind by "looking beyond the mark." That is, they missed the point. They missed the main message. In the case of the Jews, they looked beyond the mark when Christ was the mark. They focused on the minutiae of the commentary concerning the Law, when Christ was the message of the Law. They confused means with ends, tokens with covenants, ritual with religion.

Elder Dean L. Larsen offered the following insights into this unusual scriptural passage: "Jacob speaks of a people who placed themselves in serious jeopardy in spiritual things because they were unwilling to accept simple, basic principles of truth. They entertained and intrigued themselves with 'things that they could not understand' (Jacob 4:14). They were apparently afflicted with a pseudosophistication and a snobbishness that gave them a false sense of superiority over those who came among them with the Lord's words of plainness. They went beyond the mark of wisdom and prudence, and obviously failed to stay within the circle of fundamental gospel truths, which provide a basis for faith. They must have reveled in speculative and theoretical matters that obscured for them the fundamental spiritual truths."[8]

We begin the process of spiritual maturity as we come to treasure up the word of the Lord, a sure means of avoiding deception (Joseph Smith–Matthew 1:37); as we find satisfaction and great delight in poring over and discussing the fundamental doctrines of the gospel; and as we wait upon the Lord to make us into new creatures and to reveal his purposes, all in his own time, and in his own way, and according to his own will (see D&C 88:68). Truly, there are transcendent promises made to those who "continue in the faith grounded and settled, and [are] not moved away from the hope of the gospel" (Colossians 1:23).

NOTES

1. Oaks, "Family History," 6–7.
2. Smith, *Gospel Doctrine,* 122.
3. Smith, *Gospel Doctrine,* 116–17.
4. Lee, *Improvement Era,* June 1970, 63–64.
5. McConkie, *Doctrines of the Restoration,* 232.
6. Packer, *That All May Be Edified,* 338.
7. Kimball, *Faith Precedes the Miracle,* 255–56
8. Larsen, Conference Report, October 1987, 12.

CHAPTER 12

BE STILL AND KNOW

MANY YEARS AGO I HAD occasion to fly across the country and then drive throughout the Northeast with one of my teenage sons. We spent two weeks in New York, Connecticut, Massachusetts, and New Hampshire. We visited the Baseball Hall of Fame as well as the Basketball Hall of Fame and attended a New York Yankees baseball game. In addition, we visited many American history and LDS Church history sites. It was a fun and very worthwhile trip. We grew closer as father and son, and I enjoyed the restful days and the beautiful countryside.

The trip was not without its frustrations, however, as we are both human and both enjoy doing things our way. I wanted to get up early each morning and be on the road by daybreak so that we could see everything on our agenda; he wanted to sleep in and pursue our agenda well into the night, at a time when I was dragging physically. I wanted to visit my old missionary cities and apartments and tracting areas and even try to locate some of the older members of the Church in the area;

he felt that was a waste of time and preferred other, more fun things to do and see. In New York City I was eager for us to see some Broadway musicals and enjoy some cultural experiences we could receive only in the Big Apple; he wanted to see the movie *Jurassic Park,* even though we could do that anytime back home. And so forth.

Another area of difference between us had to do with how we occupied our time while we drove from city to city. There were times when I simply wanted to sit quietly or maybe even visit together. He saw it otherwise: the moment he closed the car door, he would reach forward and turn on the radio. That particular difference between us highlighted what may well be a generational difference as well. Because of the busyness of my life, I have come to treasure quiet moments, rare segments of time when I can listen to the silence, reflect on important things, and even pray. Younger people are not as inclined to want to sit quietly; in no time, they are antsy, nervous, and eager to fill the airways with music.

In recent months I have had the responsibility as a stake president to release two bishops and call new ones. There are, of course, many outstanding Latter-day Saint men in my area of the country, noble and faithful and experienced souls who could serve worthily and well. But it matters very much that the right man be called, that the Lord recommend and approve him, and that the entire stake presidency feel that comforting assurance. We had discussed several names over a period of months, all of which were fine with us. We wanted to know, however, what the Lord felt about the matter, and so we continued to talk regularly and pray periodically.

For some reason, I just couldn't get settled on two specific names. It seemed like I was always racing here or there, running to and fro in the earth—doing good things, serving righteous causes, but not pausing long enough to learn the will of God. Shauna and I traveled with some friends to England on an LDS Church history tour. About halfway through we learned that the next day would be spent in fun activities—visiting recreational areas, shopping, and so forth—and that nothing of any historical significance would be covered. I knew only too well that time was running out and that I needed to focus on the bishops to be called. I asked the group if they would mind if I stayed behind and spent the day at the hotel. They could not have cared less.

Fortunately, the hotel was located in a rural area, a few miles from a small city. When the group had left the next day, I took my scriptures and a bottle of water and walked for about half an hour until I found a beautiful, hilly area. I climbed to the top of a hill, marveled at the loveliness of the location, and sat quietly for a couple of hours. I read some chapters in the Book of Mormon, prayed earnestly for direction about who should be called as bishop, roamed about the top of the hill, and sat and listened for some time. There, in the quiet and beauty of the English countryside, all alone with my thoughts and my God, I received strong impressions about who should serve where. The still, small voice was heard; it was all very clear, very simple, very powerful. The calls were extended, the same witness of the Spirit that initiated the call accompanied us in the interviews, and some great and good things are now taking place. Lives are being blessed.

I really don't believe that we need to travel to England or drive to a farm or climb a mountain to commune more regularly with the Lord. But we do need time, and silence, and the

137

personal discipline associated with pondering, meditation, and meaningful reflection.

On an earlier trip to England, several colleagues and I spent a number of days at Oxford University and retraced the steps of C. S. Lewis. Having studied most of his writings and having read a number of biographies of his unusual life, we wanted to get a better sense of this man who had such fascinating insights into the Savior and his Atonement. We stayed at Magdalen College, ate and slept in the same quarters and pubs where Lewis had been, and conversed in some of the rooms where he had held tutorials with small groups of students. In addition, we took strolls behind the college on a pathway that Lewis traversed hundreds of times. On the flight home, I reflected on Lewis's life—his studies, his scholarship, his conversion to Christianity, and his lasting effect on the Christian world. The thought that weighed upon me was that at least as important as Lewis's broad academic training was his contemplative mind, his desire to walk and think and analyze and synthesize and distill truth.

One writer commented: "Silence, it seems, is to be filled. I suppose we inherit this sense of silence as 'dead air time' from radio and TV, where every second of time not pulsing with a voice or image is 'lost' or 'dead.' Silence, like prime time and airwaves, has become a commodity to be bought, sold, filled, framed, and obliterated: a 'nothing' that must be made into a 'something.'"[1]

Elijah discovered that Jehovah was not in the mighty wind or the fire or the earthquake but in "a still small voice" (1 Kings 19:12). Although the King James Version of this passage employs the language with which we are most familiar—and which is also used in modern revelation in Doctrine and

Covenants 85:6—the New International Version states that
Jehovah was to be known through "a gentle whisper." The New
Revised Standard Version records that the Lord was experienced as the "sound of sheer silence." That is, "the [Christian]
church's long history of contemplative practice seems to suggest that there is some knowledge of God that can come only
in stillness—silence large and long and intentional enough to
open a sacred space for the Holy One to enter."[2]

People of the world specialize in noise and busyness, while
those who yearn for closeness to the Lord hunger after silence
and peace. For many years Elder Mark E. Petersen had the
unpleasant assignment, as a member of the Quorum of the
Twelve Apostles, of dealing with apostates, with those who had
lost their way and wandered into forbidden paths. He related
more than once that in the hundreds of interviews with stray-
ing souls, almost always the wanderers expressed the thought
that they knew what they were doing was proper and right
because they had a burning in the bosom to prove it, presumably referring to the principle of revelation set forth in Doctrine
and Covenants 9:7–9. Elder Petersen commented that for the
longest time he was convinced that such sentiments were
naive, ill-informed, or just plain false. He began to realize, however, that these people were probably feeling something, perhaps even a warm or burning sensation, even though such was
not of God. He commented that although they regularly
referred to their inner burning, there was one thing no one of
them ever manifested during the interview. That one thing was
peace. Not one of them was at peace. Not one of them was at
home with himself. Not one of them evidenced the quiet confidence of the Spirit of God that they might have enjoyed had
they pursued a righteous course.

Peace. Peace is what it is all about in the gospel sense. Although most members of the Church know what peace is, I believe that as a people we have not fully appreciated what a remarkable fruit of the Spirit and what a transcendent manifestation of spiritual growth and holiness peace is. As we grow in holiness, we come to realize that peace is a priceless gift in a world that is at war with itself; we look to him who is called the Prince of Peace for our succor and support. Peace is not only a cherished commodity in the here and now but also a harbinger of glorious things yet to be (D&C 59:23). Peace is a sure and solid sign from God that the heavens are pleased. In referring to an occasion when the spirit of testimony had been given, the Master asked Oliver Cowdery: "Did I not speak peace to your mind? What greater witness can you have than from God?" (D&C 6:23).

Sin and neglect of duty result in disunity of the soul and strife and confusion and noise; repentance and forgiveness and rebirth bring quiet and rest and peace. Sin results in disorder; the Holy Spirit is an organizing principle that brings order and congruence. The world and the worldly cannot bring peace. They cannot settle the soul (D&C 101:36). "Peace, peace to him that is far off, and to him that is near, saith the Lord; and I will heal him. But the wicked are like the troubled sea, when it cannot rest, whose waters cast up mire and dirt. There is no peace, saith my God, to the wicked" (Isaiah 57:19–21).

On the other hand, the Savior said: "Peace I leave with you, my peace I give unto you: not as the world giveth, give I unto you. Let not your heart be troubled, neither let it be afraid" (John 14:27). As Paul wrote, those who have been justified by faith—who have entered into covenant with Christ, have been forgiven of their sins, and have had the Lord's righteousness

imputed unto them—have "peace with God through our Lord
Jesus Christ" (Romans 5:1). True Saints "let the peace of God
rule in [their] hearts" (Colossians 3:15). Paul elsewhere
instructs us to "be careful for nothing"—meaning, of course,
not to be overly concerned or weighed down by worry—"but
in every thing by prayer and supplication with thanksgiving let
your requests be made known unto God. And the peace of
God, which passeth all understanding, shall keep your hearts
and minds through Christ Jesus" (Philippians 4:6–7).

President David O. McKay observed that "we pay too little
attention to the value of meditation, a principle of devotion. . . .
Meditation is the language of the soul. . . . Meditation is a form
of prayer. . . . Meditation is one of the most secret, most sacred
doors through which we pass into the presence of the Lord."[3]
President McKay related to the general authorities a story of
Bishop John Wells, a member of the Presiding Bishopric, that
pointed up the need for times when we put aside our cares,
shelve our worries, and open ourselves to divine direction.
President Harold B. Lee recounted: "A son of Bishop Wells was
killed in Emigration Canyon on a railroad track. Brother John
Wells was a great detail man and prepared many of the reports
we are following up now. His boy was run over by a freight
train. Sister Wells was inconsolable. She mourned during the
three days prior to the funeral, received no comfort at the
funeral, and was in a rather serious state of mind.

"One day soon after the funeral services while she was lying
on her bed relaxed, still mourning, she said her son appeared
to her and said, 'Mother, do not mourn, do not cry. I am all
right.' He . . . explained that he had given the signal to the engi-
neer to move on, and then made the usual effort to catch the
railing on the freight train; but as he attempted to do so his foot

caught on a root and he failed to catch the handrail, and his body fell under the train. It was clearly an accident.

"Now, listen. He said that as soon as he realized that he was in another environment he tried to see his father, *but couldn't reach him. His father was so busy with the duties in his office he could not respond to his call.* Therefore he had come to his mother. He said to her, 'You tell father that all is well with me, and I want you not to mourn anymore.'

"Then the President made the statement that the point he had in mind was that when we are relaxed in a private room we are more susceptible to those things; and that so far as he was concerned, his best thoughts come after he gets up in the morning and is relaxed and thinking about the duties of the day; that impressions come more clearly, as if it were to hear a voice. Those impressions are right. If we are worried about something and upset in our feelings, the inspiration does not come. If we so live that our minds are free from worry and our conscience is clear and our feelings are right toward one another, the operation of the Spirit of the Lord upon our spirit is as real as when we pick up the telephone; but when they come, we must be brave enough to take the suggested actions."[4]

The path to holiness is a path to wholeness, a road that impels us to seek out sacred space and search for sacred moments. It is a quest for quiet time, even if such moments are few and fleeting. We are invited by the Prince of Peace to "be still, and know that I am God" (Psalm 46:10; D&C 101:16).

NOTES
1. McEntyre, "Silence Is to Dwell In," 62.
2. McEntyre, "Silence Is to Dwell In," 63.
3. McKay, *Man May Know for Himself,* 22–23.
4. *Teachings of Harold B. Lee,* 415; italics in original.

CHAPTER 13

MILK BEFORE MEAT—
BUT MEAT

WHEN SHAUNA WAS HAVING our third son, she happened to share a room in the hospital with a young mother who was there to have her second baby. This woman had gone into the hospital for the first child with no idea of what to expect. After being in the hospital for an extended time, she overheard a nurse whisper that they might have to induce labor. The young woman thought that meant they might need to put her to death to save the baby, so she promptly and quietly got out of bed, dressed herself, and went home. The baby was delivered at home by a neighbor.

This young woman was now back to give birth to her second baby. As they talked together, my wife commented that it was a bit of a financial challenge to buy extra food items. The young woman replied, "We always fed our baby what the rest of us ate."

Shauna asked, "What do you mean?"

"Well, if we had chicken, the baby had chicken. If we had

potatoes, the baby had potatoes. If we had beans, the baby had beans."

My wife asked, "You mean when the child was a little older?"

"No," she said, "when we brought the baby home."

Shauna asked delicately, "Is he, uh, still living? Is he all right now?"

The young mother answered, "Oh, yes, he gained twenty pounds in no time at all."

There's a lesson there. Some foods are not only inappropriate but dangerous for an infant to eat. So it is with our spiritual digestive system and our growth to spiritual maturity. Just as it would be unwise for a college student who had very little math in high school to jump into an integral calculus class, so too must we be careful about what we study, how we study, and when we study. There is, in a manner of speaking, a system of gospel prerequisites. Elder Boyd K. Packer explained: "Teaching prematurely or at the wrong time some things that are true can invite sorrow and heartbreak instead of the joy intended to accompany learning. . . .

"The scriptures teach emphatically that we must give milk before meat. The Lord made it very clear that some things are to be given only to those who are worthy.

"It matters very much not only *what* we are told but *when* we are told it."[1]

The Savior taught that gospel prerequisistes should be observed when teaching or learning sacred things (Matthew 7:6–7). After having spoken of the profound truths associated with his own suffering in Gethsemane and thus of our need to repent, the Lord warned: "And I command you that you preach naught but repentance, and show not these things unto the world until it is wisdom in me. For they cannot bear meat now, but milk they must receive; wherefore, they must not know these things, lest they perish" (D&C 19:21–22). A person who knows very little about our doctrine, for example, will probably not understand or appreciate our teachings concerning temples, sealing powers, eternal life, or the potential godhood of man.

The Prophet Joseph Smith observed, "If we start right, it is easy to go right all the time; but if we start wrong, we may go wrong, and it [will] be a hard matter to get right."[2] When a proper foundation has been laid, the truth can then flow more freely. The apostle Peter is said to have explained to Clement of Rome: "The teaching of all doctrine has a certain order, and there are some things which must be delivered first, others in the second place, and others in the third, and so all in their order; and if these things be delivered in their order, they become plain; but if they be brought forward out of order, they will seem to be spoken against reason."[3]

After I had been on my mission for about fifteen months, I was assigned to work in a beautiful section of Connecticut. My companion, a nice fellow to be sure, had one problem that affected the work somewhat—his mind was never with us. He always seemed to be off in another world. One day in early summer we arrived at the door of a small but lovely home. A woman who appeared to be about thirty-five years old opened her door and unlatched the screen door. "Yes? Is there something I can do for you?"

It was Elder Jackson's turn to be the spokesman. "We're missionaries for The Church of Jesus Christ of Latter-day Saints, sometimes called the Mormons. We have a message about Christ we would like to share with you."

She looked us over very carefully. "I don't think so. I have my own faith."

My companion, who probably wasn't paying attention to what she said, went silent. After waiting uncomfortably for at least ten or fifteen seconds, I blurted out, "And which church do you attend?"

She came right back: "I didn't say I attended a church—I said I had my own faith."

Somewhat surprised, I responded, "Could you tell us about your faith?"

"I don't think I want to," she said. "You would make fun of me."

I assured her we would not. "What is your faith?" I asked.

"Well," she timidly declared, "I believe the physical body is the temple of God and that people ought to take better care of their bodies. For example, I think it's wrong for people to smoke or drink." I commented that we felt her thinking was right on the mark.

She continued, "Well, there's more. I don't drink coffee or tea." Then she asked, "What do the Mormons believe?"

It was difficult for me not to speak out, but I felt I ought to allow Elder Jackson to engage what was obviously a great teaching moment. I could almost see the wheels in his mental machinery turning. He answered, "Well, we believe in baptism for the dead." The woman carefully pulled the screen door shut and latched it. Before closing the main door she said, with a pained look on her face, "That sounds sick."

I had some idea of what she was thinking and of how bizarre these Latter-day Saints appeared to be. Mostly I was stunned. Before we left the porch, I turned to Elder Jackson and asked in utter disbelief, "What were you doing?"

He seemed offended. "We do believe in baptism for the dead, don't we?"

"Yes, we do, Elder Jackson. So why didn't you tell her about polygamy?"

His response was even more stunning. "I thought about doing that next, but she closed the door."

"Elder," I said, "this lady lives the Word of Wisdom."

"I thought that was odd," he replied as we walked to the next door.

This woman had essentially answered the door with her tin cup and said, "I thirst." We had answered, "We can fix that," and proceeded to drag out the fire hose and drown her in the living waters. It wasn't that the woman was not bright enough to understand the concept of salvation for the dead. The problem was that we had not laid a proper doctrinal foundation, and reflecting Peter's words, our message seemed to be spoken against reason.

There is indeed a system of gospel prerequisites. Milk must come before meat. As we grow in holiness, it is vital that we grow steadily and surely, feeding regularly and consistently upon the fundamental and foundational doctrines of salvation. Too often members of the Church, supposing that they are deeper and stronger than they really are, make an effort to feast upon heavy meat—doctrinal matters that are clearly beyond the purview of what is taught by the Brethren today—well before they are ready to do so. A friend who served as a bishop indicated that after a member of his ward—a good man but one who had wrestled for years with the Word of Wisdom— had attended a series of discussions on unusually deep doctrines, he had said, "Bishop, I'm convinced that if I can simply

make my calling and election sure, I can then get the strength
to stop smoking!"

What's wrong with this picture? Only the order of things,
that's all. My experience has been that people who want to
spend their time studying materials beyond the standard
works, who feel that the scriptures and the words of living
prophets are too elementary for them, are usually spiritually
unstable, and their influence for good is minimal. They generally do more to sow discord in a ward than they do to build
unity and strengthen the Saints.

The prophets and apostles have a much clearer perspective
on what should and should not be taught than most of us will
ever have. By traveling throughout the earth and meeting regularly with the Saints, they sense the "bearing capacity" of the
people, what we are and are not prepared to receive. We would
do well to use the teachings of the general authorities as a
gauge of the readiness of the people. As we read through the
Book of Mormon, we come face to face with this principle: "It
came to pass that Alma, having authority from God, ordained
priests; even one priest to every fifty of their number did he
ordain to preach unto them, and to teach them concerning the
things pertaining to the kingdom of God. And he commanded
them that they should teach nothing save it were the things
which he had taught" (Mosiah 18:18–19). The same book
records: "Therefore they did assemble themselves together in
different bodies, being called churches; every church having
their priests and their teachers, and every priest preaching the
word according as it was delivered to him by the mouth of
Alma" (Mosiah 25:21). In our day the revelations declare, "And
let them"—John Corrill and John Murdock—"journey from
thence preaching the word by the way, saying none other

things than that which the prophets and apostles have written, and that which is taught them by the Comforter through the prayer of faith" (D&C 52:9).

On the other hand, while we must see to it that our growth in understanding is steady and sustained, we must be stretching, expanding our views, and opening our minds to new truths and new applications. That is, we need to partake of milk before meat, but eventually we need meat. "For when for the time ye ought to be teachers," Paul wrote, "ye have need that one teach you again which be the first principles of the oracles of God; and are become such as have need of milk, and not of strong meat. For every one that useth milk is unskilful in the word of righteousness: for he is a babe. But strong meat belongeth to them that are of full age"—or in other words are mature—"even those who by reason of use have their senses exercised to discern both good and evil" (Hebrews 5:12–14).

It is not uncommon to teach returned missionaries in a Book of Mormon class, perhaps two or three weeks into the semester, and hear one of the group respond to something I have taught with "Hey! Wait a minute. How can that be true? I've never heard that!" The implication is fascinating—if the student hasn't encountered this particular idea before, it can't be true.

We must be willing to think, to open ourselves to new insights, to broaden our scope, if we truly desire to make a difference in the kingdom of God in the years ahead. It is one thing to respond to a hard question by saying, "I don't know the answer to your question, but I know the gospel is true." That's a noble approach, I suppose. If we don't know, then we don't know. We ought not try to bluff our way through things. And it's good to know the work is true, despite what we don't know. But how much more powerful is an answer like this one: "That's a good question. Let me answer your question first, and then let me bear my testimony of the truths associated with this matter." The Lord and his Church desperately need members who are committed to the faith and have a testimony of the gospel. But of even greater worth are those who know the gospel is true and also know the gospel.

President Joseph F. Smith explained that "the voicing of one's testimony, however eloquently phrased or beautifully expressed, is no fit or acceptable substitute for the needed discourse of instruction and counsel expected in a general gathering of the people. The man who professes a testimony as herein described, and who assumes that his testimony embraces all the knowledge he needs, and who therefore lives in indolence and ignorance shall surely discover his error to his own cost and loss." And then comes this poignant message: "Of those who speak in his name, the Lord requires humility, not ignorance."[4]

Elder B. H. Roberts said: "In no department is the frank and honest confession 'I don't know,' more imperative than in Theology; and when it is given as an actual confession of having reached the limits of our knowledge, it is worthy of all praise. But if it becomes tainted with the spirit of 'I don't care,' then I have no respect for it. . . . Achievement in divine things, progress in the knowledge of them, comes only with hard striving, earnest endeavor, determined seeking.

"Mental laziness is the vice of men, especially with reference to divine things." Elder Roberts continued: "Men seem to think that because inspiration and revelation are factors in connection with the things of God, therefore the pain and stress of mental effort are not required; that by some means these elements act somewhat as Elijah's ravens and feed us without effort on our part. . . . Just now it is much in fashion to laud 'the simple faith'; which is content to believe without understanding, or even without much effort to understand. . . . I maintain that 'simple faith'—which is so often ignorant and simpering acquiescence, and not faith at all—but simple faith taken at its highest value, which is faith without understanding of the thing believed, is not equal to intelligent faith, the faith that is the gift of God, supplemented by earnest endeavor to find through prayerful thought and search a rational ground for faith—for acceptance of truth; and hence the duty of striving for a rational faith in which the intellect as well as the heart—the feeling—has a place and is a factor."[5]

Because we do not dispense large portions of meat (or because my students are not receiving the same in class) does not mean that we should not personally be striving for deeper understanding; the gap between what we are learning and what we teach may well grow larger as the years go by. The portion of the word to be given to the Saints may not change appreciably, but we shouldn't always be teaching on the edge of our knowledge.

In recent years the Brethren have pleaded with the Saints to teach the gospel, to focus on doctrine, to emphasize substance, to stress the principles and precepts that lead to a change of heart and growth and salvation. The Lord instructed the early Saints to "teach the principles of my gospel, which are in the Bible and the Book of Mormon, in the which is the fulness of the gospel" (D&C 42:12). We have been told that "when ye are assembled together ye shall instruct and edify each other, that ye may know how to act and direct my church, how to act upon the points of my law and commandments, which I have given" (D&C 43:8). We are to "teach one another the doctrine of the kingdom. Teach ye diligently," the Savior has implored, "and my grace shall attend you" (D&C 88:77–78). "True doctrine, understood, changes attitudes and behavior," Elder Boyd K. Packer declared. "The study of the doctrines of the gospel will improve behavior quicker than a study of behavior will improve behavior."[6]

There is a discipline imposed on those called to lead or teach in the Church to use time wisely and to see that what is said and done in our meetings leads to enrichment, edification, and spiritual growth. Not many years ago, while serving in a stake presidency, I stole away from stake assignments to attend a Sunday School Gospel Doctrine class. The reading was Acts 19 and Paul's epistle to the Galatians. I was excited, because I knew something about those remarkable chapters of the New Testament and anticipated that we could indeed have a marvelous experience in class that day. But my hopes were soon dashed, for the instructor opened the class by saying, "Now, before we get to our topic, let me tell you about a recent trip my wife and I took to Hawaii." For the next forty minutes the teacher spoke of swimming and snorkeling and pineapple and fishing. Just as it was time to close, he asked, "What does all of this have to do with the apostle Paul?" The silence was deafening. Clearly, our time had been wasted by a man who was unprepared to teach that day. It would have been far more enjoyable and worthwhile simply to read selected passages and invite comments on the material from class members. Many of us went to Church hungry that day but returned home largely unfed.

Elder Bruce R. McConkie described our responsibility as teachers and students in the quest for mutual edification: "We come into these congregations, and sometimes a speaker brings a jug of living water that has in it many gallons. And when he pours it out on the congregation, all the members have brought is a single cup and so that's all they take away. Or maybe they have their hands over the cups, and they don't get anything to speak of.

"On other occasions we have meetings where the speaker comes and all he brings is a little cup of eternal truth, and the members of the congregation come with a large jug, and all they get in their jugs is the little dribble that came from a man who should have known better and who should have prepared himself and talked from the revelations and spoken by the power of the Holy Spirit. We are obligated in the Church to speak by the power of the Spirit. We are commanded to treasure up the words of light and truth and then give forth the portion that is appropriate and needful on every occasion."[7]

Not long after Shauna and I were married, we moved into a new ward. In priesthood meeting the instructor of the high priests group said, "Look, guys, we all know this stuff that's in the manuals, as well as the stories in scripture; we've been over it again and again. I propose that we grow up and move on to discussions of things that really matter." I smiled inside, because I sensed then—and I know it ever so much more surely today—that the scriptures and the words of the prophets have an eternal relevance and thus a life of their own. Each one of us brings to our most recent reading of scripture new challenges, new accomplishments, new insights, and hopefully new eyes that now see more clearly than the last time we engaged that particular passage. Constant review of basic principles constantly brings increased spiritual insight. We reduce the realm of the unknown not by wandering in it but by feasting on our knowledge of that which God has already revealed. A vital key to individual revelation is institutional revelation.

No matter the depth of our personal searching after the meat of the plan of salvation, true spiritual maturity will be manifest in our continued return to the milk that provided substance for our souls in our formative years. I have a love and depth of appreciation for the scriptures now that I simply could not have understood thirty years ago. I treasure the words of living apostles and prophets today as silver and gold. In addition, the people I admire the most, the men and women I consider to be some of the finest teachers in the Church, are people who, despite their breadth and their depth, are devoted to the standard works of the Church and have a great desire to teach the portion of the word the Lord has allotted for us today. For them, as for those they teach so ably and well, the simple has become profound.

I think I would be correct in suggesting that the institutional Church is not responsible to teach very much meat; the Church teaches largely the milk of the gospel. Thus, it's foolish for members of the Church to become either disenchanted or discouraged because they aren't hearing deep doctrine preached in sacrament meeting or receiving new historical or doctrinal truth in Sunday School each week. The Church is, in many ways, like a university, a place where a person should learn to learn. We need not find fault with the Church if things are too simply presented or if matters seem repetitious. The gaining of meat becomes an individual responsibility, a personal quest. "God's earthly kingdom is a school in which his saints learn the doctrines of salvation. Some members of the Church are being taught elementary courses; others are approaching graduation and can do independent research where the deep and hidden things are concerned. All must learn line upon line and precept upon precept."[8]

Let us consider what might be called the parable of the hidden treasure. The kingdom of heaven is like a man who learned of pearls of great price buried in a field. With joy and anticipation he began his search for the priceless gems. After barely breaking the surface of the ground, he came upon a valuable stone, one which later brought substantial material gain. The man led his friends to the field, and other stones of like worth were uncovered, all barely beneath the surface of the ground. Indeed, as often as a person chose to drop his trowel or hand spade into the now well-furrowed field, he was almost assured of a valuable find.

Then one day a certain man went to the field alone, a man who had previously uncovered many valuable stones. As he sank his shovel into the earth and pushed beneath the accustomed level of digging, he happened upon a larger variety of stones and many gems of even greater value. Upon telling of his discovery, many were heard to say, "We have enough! Are these our stones not of great worth? Are they not to be had through digging near the surface?"

A few of his friends, however, rejoiced with him in his prize and sought the same with eagerness. These made the extra effort to dig deeper, made similar finds, and were richly rewarded.

Blessed is that man who seeks deep to find and know the word: unto him is given the "greater portion of the word, until it is given unto him to know the mysteries of God until he know them in full" (Alma 12:10).

NOTES

1. Packer, *Let Not Your Heart Be Troubled,* 107–8; italics in original.
2. *Teachings of the Prophet Joseph Smith,* 343.

3. "Clementine Recognitions," III, 34; cited in Nibley, *Since Cumorah*, 97.

4. Smith, *Gospel Doctrine*, 206.

5. Roberts, *Seventy's Course in Theology*, 5:iv–v.

6. Packer, Conference Report, October 1986, 20.

7. McConkie, "Seven Deadly Heresies," 80.

8. McConkie, *Doctrinal New Testament Commentary*, 2:324.

CHAPTER 14

FEAR AND TREMBLING

I T HAS BEEN MY OPPORTUNITY over the last couple of decades to travel to many different places throughout the world. Because much of my focus professionally has been in the area of religion and worship, I have enjoyed visiting some of the most beautiful churches and cathedrals ever built by mortal man. Although pomp and ceremony do not impress me, I have been stirred by the way men and women of past centuries have sought to point us, literally and symbolically, toward the God and Father of us all.

It has occurred to me more than once that we as a people do not "do awe" very well. That is, we are a very functional and focused bunch, and we tend to place great emphasis on serving others, doing the work of the kingdom, and involving ourselves in the betterment of society. We are less likely to ponder, reflect, and open ourselves to feelings of wonder, awe, and praise. Yet this element of the spiritual experience, this dimension of holiness, is a deeply significant and rewarding one. The experience of awe is an experience of wonder, acknowledgment, humility, and gratitude. It is a recognition of who God is, what he has done for us, and who we are in relation to him.

To stand before our Maker with fear and trembling is to stand before him in honest acknowledgment of his majesty and power; to stand before him in overwhelming humility and sobering recognition of the distance between a wholly perfect immortal being and an oh-so-imperfect mortal being; to stand before him in gratitude and thanksgiving, confessing fully his hand in all that is good and true and beautiful. To fear him is to reverence him. To tremble before him is, on the one hand, to state categorically that his is the capacity to smite with the breath of his lips and bring to an end our second estate; on the other hand, it is to be staggered and sweetened by his love and mercy and divine condescension.

We have been commanded to worship God the Eternal Father, in the name of Jesus Christ, by the power of the Holy Ghost (2 Nephi 25:16; Jacob 4:5; D&C 20:29), to worship "in spirit and in truth: for the Father seeketh such to worship him" (John 4:23). In speaking of how we come unto the Savior, Nephi explained that "the right way is to believe in Christ, and deny him not; and Christ is the Holy One of Israel; wherefore ye must bow down before him, and worship him with all your might, mind, and strength, and your whole soul; and if ye do this ye shall in nowise be cast out" (2 Nephi 25:29).

What does it mean to worship God or to worship Christ? What is worship? How do we do it? The dictionary defines *worship* as "reverent honor and homage paid to God or a sacred personage," "formal or ceremonious rendering of such honor and homage," or "adoring reverence or regard."[1] Elder Bruce R. McConkie wrote that "the forms of worship are many. Prayers, sermons, testimonies, gospel ordinances, attendance at church meetings, doing missionary service, visiting the fatherless and the widows in their afflictions, and a great many other things are all part of pure religion and true worship."[2]

But there is more. That additional ingredient of pure worship is set forth in a revelation given through the Prophet Joseph Smith on 6 May 1833. Verses 6 through 18 of the revelation we know as Doctrine and Covenants 93 are essentially an excerpt of the messianic testimony and written record of John the Baptist.[3] After bearing witness of Christ as the Light and Redeemer, the Word or messenger of salvation, the Spirit of truth, and the Creator, the account continues: "And I, John, bear record that I beheld his glory, as the glory of the Only Begotten of the Father, full of grace and truth, even the Spirit of truth, which came and dwelt in the flesh, and dwelt among us. And I, John, saw that he [Jesus] received not of the fulness [of the glory of the Father] at the first, but received grace for grace."

The Master did not dissipate his power or diminish his strength in any way through extending himself in constant service to others. As he gave and gave and gave of himself, he received richer and grander endowments of divine assistance, of enabling power from above. "And he received not of the fulness at first, but continued from grace to grace, until he received a fulness" (D&C 93:11–13). That the Savior grew from grace to grace implies a developmental process, a progression from one level of spiritual attainment to a higher, until in the resurrection he received a fulness of the glory and power of the Father.[4] The scripture continues: "And I, John, bear record that he received a fulness of the glory of the Father; and he received all power, both in heaven and on earth, and the glory of the Father was with him, for he dwelt in him. And it shall come to pass, that if you are faithful you shall receive the fulness of the record of John." Now note this language: "I give unto you these sayings that you may understand and know how to worship, and know what [or Who] you worship, that you may come unto the Father in my name, and in due time receive of his fulness" (D&C 93:16–19).

Thus we see that true worship consists in the emulation of God or, more specifically, the imitation of Christ. We worship him in that we learn of him and of his ways; we study his life and his teachings; we marvel at and seek to acquire his godly attributes; and we strive to come unto the Father, through the Son, and eventually receive a fulness. We serve others as he served. We give of ourselves as he did. He "went about doing good" (Acts 10:38), and so should we. He took up his cross in that he denied himself of all ungodliness and worldly lusts (JST Matthew 16:26), and so must we endeavor to do. "For if you keep my commandments you shall receive of his [the Father's] fulness, and be glorified in me as I am in the Father; therefore, I say unto you, you shall receive grace for grace" (D&C 93:20).

In short, we worship the Lord in that we honor him and strive to pattern our lives after him. In the School of the Prophets, Joseph Smith asked: "Where shall we find a proto-type into whose likeness we may be assimilated, in order that we may be made partakers of life and salvation? or in other words, where shall we find a saved being? for if we can find a saved being, we may ascertain without much difficulty what all others must be in order to be saved. We think that it will not be a matter of dispute . . . among those who believe the Bible, that it is Christ; all will agree in this, that *he is the prototype or standard of salvation;* or, in other words, that he is a saved being. And if we should continue our interrogation, and ask how it is that he is saved? the answer would be—because *he is a just and holy being.*"⁵

I have thought about this a great deal, wondering what other factors might contribute to our difficulty in feeling a deeper sense of reverence and awe toward Deity. Perhaps Latter-day Saints have a challenge in this vein because of the knowledge restored through the Prophet Joseph concerning God—that He is a person, a personal being, a glorified, exalted Man of Holiness (Moses 6:57). Does the fact that God was not always God affect our view of him and thus our capacity to bow reverently before him? Such truths, if properly grasped, should cause us to love and honor and feel wonder toward our Heavenly Father.

Joseph Smith's first vision represents the beginning of the revelation of God to man in this dispensation. We will no doubt spend a lifetime seeking to understand the doctrinal profundity of that theophany. This appearance of the Father and Son in upstate New York had the effect of challenging those creeds of Christendom out of which the doctrine of the Trinity evolved—a doctrine that had evolved from efforts to reconcile Christian theology with Greek philosophy. President Gordon B. Hinckley observed: "To me it is a significant and marvelous thing that in establishing and opening this dispensation our Father did so with a revelation of himself and of his Son Jesus Christ, as if to say to all the world that he was weary of the attempts of men, earnest though these attempts might have been, to define and describe him. . . . The experience of Joseph Smith in a few moments in the grove on a spring day in 1820, brought more light and knowledge and understanding of the personality and reality and substance of God and his Beloved Son than men had arrived at during centuries of speculation."⁶

By revelation Joseph Smith came to know that the Father, the Son, and the Holy Ghost constitute the Godhead. From the beginning the Prophet Joseph taught that the members of the Godhead are one in purpose, one in mind, one in glory, one in attributes and powers, but separate persons.[7]

God is the Father of the spirits of all men and women (Numbers 16:22; 27:16), the source of light and truth, the embodiment of all godly attributes and gifts, and the supreme power and intelligence over all things. From the book of Moses, we learn that among the ancients God the Father was called Man of Holiness, and thus his Only Begotten Son is the Son of Man of Holiness, or the Son of Man (Moses 6:57). The title Man of Holiness opens to us a deeper understanding of Deity. We believe that God the Father is an exalted man, a corporeal being, a personage of flesh and bones. That God has a physical body is one of the most important of all truths restored in this dispensation; it is inextricably tied to such doctrines as the immortality of the soul, the literal resurrection, eternal marriage, and the continuation of the family unit into eternity. In his corporeal, or physical, nature, God can be in only one place at a time. His divine nature is such, however, that his glory, his power, and his influence, meaning his Holy Spirit, fills the immensity of space and is the means by which he is omnipresent and through which law and light and life are extended to us (D&C 88:6–13). The Father's physical body does not limit his capacity or detract one whit from his infinite holiness any more than Christ's resurrected body did so (Luke 24; John 20–21). Interestingly enough, research indicates that the idea of God's corporeality was taught in the early Christian church into the fourth and fifth centuries, before being lost to the knowledge of the people.[8]

On the one hand, we worship a divine Being with whom we can identify. That is to say, his infinity does not preclude either his immediacy or his intimacy. "In the day that God created man," the scriptures attest, "in the likeness of God made he him; in the image of his own body, male and female, created he them" (Moses 6:8–9). God is not simply a spirit influence, a force in the universe, or the First Great Cause; when we pray, "Our Father which art in heaven" (Matthew 6:9), we mean what we say. We believe God is comprehendible, knowable, approachable, and, like his Beloved Son, "touched with the feeling of our infirmities" (Hebrews 4:15).

On the other hand, our God is God. There is no knowledge of which the Father is ignorant and no power he does not possess (1 Nephi 7:12; 2 Nephi 9:20; Mosiah 4:9; Alma 26:35; Helaman 9:41; Ether 3:4). Scriptural passages that speak of him being the same yesterday, today, and forever (Psalm 102:27; Hebrews 1:12; 13:8; 1 Nephi 10:18–19; 2 Nephi 27:23; Alma 7:20; Mormon 9:8–11, 19; Moroni 8:18; 10:7; D&C 3:2; 20:12, 17; 35:1) clearly have reference to his divine attributes—his love, justice, constancy, and willingness to bless his children. In addition President Joseph Fielding Smith explained that "from eternity to eternity means from the spirit existence through the probation which we are in, and then back again to the eternal existence which will follow. Surely this is everlasting, for when we receive the resurrection, we will never die. We all existed in the first eternity. I think I can say of myself and others, we are from eternity; and we will be to eternity everlasting, if we receive the exaltation."[9]

Although we know from modern revelation that godhood comes through the receipt of eternal life (D&C 132:19–20), we do not believe we will ever, worlds without end, unseat or oust

God the Eternal Father or his Only Begotten Son, Jesus Christ; those holy beings are and forever will be the Gods we worship. Even though we believe in the ultimate deification of man, I am unaware of any authoritative statement in LDS literature that suggests we will ever worship any being other than the ones within the Godhead. We believe in "one God" in the sense that we love and serve one Godhead, one divine presidency, each of whom possesses all of the attributes of Godhood (Alma 11:44; D&C 20:28). God is deserving of all of our worship, adoration, and devotion, and then some.

In an eagerness to draw closer to Christ, some members of the Church have begun to cross a sacred line, going beyond the reverential barrier that must be observed by true followers of the Christ. They speak of Jesus as though he were their next door neighbor, their buddy or chum, their pal. That is not the way to intimacy with the Savior. Oddly enough, strangely enough, it is not through humanizing Jesus, through trying to make him one of the boys, that we draw close to him and incorporate his saving powers; rather, it is through recognizing his Godhood, his divinity, his unspeakable power. In short, the more we sense his greatness, his infinity, his capacity to transform the human soul, and our utter helplessness without him, the more we come unto him. Remember, it is through the recognition of our own nothingness and weakness that strength is derived (Mosiah 2:20–21; 4:11–12, 26).

This consideration is somewhat related to our tendency to speak of Jesus as our Elder Brother. He is, of course, our Elder Brother in that he was the firstborn spirit child of God in the premortal existence. But it is of interest that the Book of Mormon prophets never speak of Jehovah as our Elder Brother. Rather, he is the Almighty God, the Eternal Judge, the Holy

One of Israel, the Holy Messiah, the Everlasting Father, the Father of heaven and of earth, the God of nature, the Supreme Being, the Keeper of the gate, the King of heaven, and the Lord God Omnipotent.

Elder M. Russell Ballard explained: "We occasionally hear some members refer to Jesus as our Elder Brother, which is a true concept based on our understanding of the premortal life with our Father in Heaven. But like many points of gospel doctrine, that simple truth doesn't go far enough in terms of describing the Savior's role in our present lives and His great position as a member of the Godhead. Thus, some non-LDS Christians are uncomfortable with what they perceive as a secondary role for Christ in our theology. They feel that we view Jesus as a spiritual peer. They believe that we view Christ as an implementor, if you will, for God but that we don't view Him as God to us and to all mankind, which, of course, is counter to biblical testimony about Christ's divinity. Let me help us understand, with clarity and testimony, our belief about Jesus Christ. We declare He is the King of Kings, Lord of Lords, the Creator, the Savior, the Captain of our Salvation, the Bright and Morning Star. He has taught us that He is in all things, above all things, through all things and round about all things, that He is Alpha and Omega, the Lord of the Universe, the first and the last relative to our salvation, and that His name is above every name and is in fact the only name under heaven by which we can be saved. . . .

"[We] can understand why some Latter-day Saints have tended to focus on Christ's Sonship as opposed to His Godhood. As members of earthly families, we can relate to Him as a child, as a Son, and as a Brother because we know how that feels. We can personalize that relationship because we ourselves are children, sons and daughters, brothers and sisters. For some it may be more difficult to relate to Him as a God. And so in an attempt to draw closer to Christ and to cultivate warm and personal feelings toward Him, some tend to humanize Him, sometimes at the expense of acknowledging His Divinity. So let us be very clear on this point: it is true that Jesus was our Elder Brother in the premortal life, but we believe that in this life it is crucial that we become 'born again' as His sons and daughters in the gospel covenant."[10]

Those who have come to know the Lord best—the prophets or covenant spokesmen—are also those who speak of him in reverent tones, who, like Isaiah, find themselves crying out, "Woe is me! For I am undone; because I am a man of unclean lips, and I dwell in the midst of a people of unclean lips: for mine eyes have seen the King, the Lord of hosts" (Isaiah 6:5). Coming into the presence of the Almighty is no light thing; we feel to respond soberly to God's command to Moses: "Put off thy shoes from off thy feet, for the place whereon thou standest is holy ground" (Exodus 3:5). Moses the Lawgiver was caught up into the immediate presence of God, beheld mighty visions of the cosmos, and then was left unto himself. "And it came to pass that it was for the space of many hours before Moses did again receive his natural strength like unto man; and he said unto himself: Now, for this cause I know that man is nothing, which thing I never had supposed. But now mine own eyes have beheld God; but not my natural, but my spiritual eyes, for my natural eyes could not have beheld; for I should have withered and died in his presence; but his glory was upon me; and I beheld his face, for I was transfigured before him" (Moses 1:10–11).

It has been my experience that as we grow in our sense of

awe toward our Heavenly Father and his Beloved Son, we concurrently grow in our reverence for the creations of God. We find ourselves more fascinated with and interested in people, more compassionate and loving toward them, and more eager to understand their challenges and struggles. Not long ago I walked along the streets of New York City. As hordes of people made their way to work—hundreds of thousands of them, black and white, male and female—I reflected on what I was witnessing: "These are all God's children. Every one of them is a son or daughter of the same God. He loves that old misshapen man and that thinly clad woman as much as he loves me. These are my brothers and sisters. We lived together before we were born. We left our first estate with such hope, such promise, such possibility. Each one of us, in his or her own way, wants desperately to be happy, to be appreciated, to make some small contribution to life here, to leave the world a better place somehow." Such an experience may be common to most people, but it has not been common to me. I wish it happened more frequently, because it stretches my soul, awakening me to realities above and beyond my own concerns.

As it is with people, so I believe it is with everything about us: as we grow in appreciation for the Creator, so do we grow in appreciation for the creation. The Spirit of the Lord has a calming effect upon our hearts, a settling and harmonizing effect upon our associations with all of God's creations. President Joseph F. Smith spoke of the influence of the Spirit on him: "The feeling that came upon me was pure peace, of love and of light. I felt in my soul that if I had sinned—and surely I was not without sin—that it had been forgiven me; that I was indeed cleansed from sin; my heart was touched, and I felt that I would not injure the smallest insect beneath my feet.

I felt as if I wanted to do good everywhere to everybody and to everything. I felt a newness of life, a newness of desire to do that which was right."[11]

It is my conviction that as we grow in holiness we find ourselves losing those feelings of enmity between us and the beasts, discarding bloodthirstiness and any yearning for wanton taking of life. At the same time, we begin to sense our stewardship to care for and tend and protect the earth. Further, scenes of bloodshed or murder, unkind treatment, crudeness, harshness, and insensitivity to people's feelings—these all become more and more repugnant to us. We discover that we are not just concerned about whether this movie or that play has explicit sexual content; we are also attentive to the level of violence in a medium, as well as the unnecessary and spiritually desensitizing influence of man's inhumanity to man. Tenderness, compassion, gentility—such are signs of spiritual growth.

While we must, on the one hand, be fully aware of the evils of our time, ever vigilant to the creeping corruption and raging relativism of the day, we must not allow ourselves to become prey to cynicism, which is an enemy to spirituality. Just after the scandal of Watergate, when the United States of America was at an all-time low in confidence in government and officials, Elder Bruce R. McConkie lifted his voice to the members of the Church: "I desire, if I may be so guided, to counsel the Latter-day Saints to take an affirmative, wholesome attitude toward world and national conditions; to turn their backs on everything that is evil and destructive; to look for that which is good and edifying in all things; to praise the Lord for his goodness and grace in giving us the glories and wonders of his everlasting gospel.

"In view of all that prevails in the world, it might be easy to center our attention on negative or evil things, or to dissipate our energies on causes and enterprises of doubtful worth and questionable productivity. . . .

"I think the Latter-day Saints have a great obligation pressing in upon them to rejoice in the Lord, to praise him for his goodness and grace, to ponder his eternal truths in their hearts, and to set their hearts on righteousness." Elder McConkie then quoted two key passages of scripture that have particular relevance to our discussion. Jehovah, in speaking through Isaiah, asked: "Who among us shall dwell with the devouring fire? Who among us shall dwell with everlasting burnings?" He answered: "He that walketh righteously, and speaketh uprightly; he that despiseth the gain of oppressions, that shaketh his hands from holding of bribes, that stoppeth his ears from hearing of blood, and shutteth his eyes from seeing evil; he shall dwell on high" (Isaiah 33:14–16). "There is an eternal law," Elder McConkie continued, "ordained by God himself before the foundations of the world, that every man shall reap as he sows. If we think evil thoughts, our tongues will utter unclean sayings. If we speak words of wickedness, we shall end up doing the works of wickedness. If our minds are centered on the carnality and evil of the world, then worldliness and unrighteousness will seem to us to be the normal way of life. If we ponder things related to sex immorality in our minds, we will soon think everybody is immoral and unclean and it will break down the barrier between us and the world. . . .

"On the other hand, if we are pondering in our hearts the things of righteousness, we shall become righteous."[12]

A second passage of scripture that has special appeal to me is from the apostle Paul: "Whatsoever things are true, whatsoever things are honest, whatsoever things are just, whatsoever things are pure, whatsoever things are lovely, whatsoever things are of good report; if there be any virtue, and if there be any praise, think on these things" (Philippians 4:8).

One way to render praise to our God, available to each one of us, is through the singing of hymns. We need not be trained professionally nor even have a particularly pleasing voice to sing. We need only a desire to express the deepest sentiments of our soul. The First Presidency has written that "the hymns invite the Spirit of the Lord, create a feeling of reverence, unify us as members, and provide a way for us to offer praises to the Lord.

"Some of the greatest sermons are preached by the singing of hymns. Hymns move us to repentance and good works, build testimony and faith, comfort the weary, console the mourning, and inspire us to endure to the end."[13]

How often we have found ourselves awed by the majesty of our Maker as we sing the words of "How Great Thou Art" or "I Stand All Amazed" or "Glory to God on High." It is often the case these days that I have difficulty making it completely through some of the sacred hymns or anthems of the Restoration without succumbing to feelings of profound gratitude and praise.

An interesting commandment in scripture is this: "Thou shalt thank the Lord thy God in all things" (D&C 59:7). Does God need the thanks? Is he somehow bettered or empowered when his children thank him? I think not. God is an independent being, and, although he loves us perfectly and desires us to be faithful and obedient, his Godhood does not depend on our doing so. Rather, our expression of thanks and gratitude is for *our* good; such declarations focus us away from ourselves and our own accomplishments and direct our thoughts to him who is the Father of Lights and the giver of all good gifts. Only through forgetting self and yielding our hearts to him can we have joy here and eternal reward and glory hereafter. Thus, "in nothing doth man offend God, or against none is his wrath kindled, save those who confess not his hand in all things, and obey not his commandments" (D&C 59:21). Consequently, "he that receiveth of God, let him account it of God" (D&C 50:34).

In that spirit our hearts should ring out in praise to the King Emmanuel: "Worthy is the Lamb that was slain to receive power, and riches, and wisdom, and strength, and honour, and glory, and blessing"; truly, "blessing, and honour, and glory, and power, be unto him that sitteth upon the throne, and unto the Lamb for ever and ever" (Revelation 5:12–13).

NOTES

1. *Random House College Dictionary,* s.v. "worship."
2. McConkie, *Promised Messiah,* 566–67.
3. John Taylor, *Mediation and Atonement,* 55; Orson Pratt, *Journal of Discourses,* 16:58; McConkie, *Doctrinal New Testament Commentary,* 1:70–71.
4. Smith, *Doctrines of Salvation,* 2:269; McConkie, *Mormon Doctrine,* 333.
5. Smith, *Lectures on Faith,* 7:9; italics added.
6. *Teachings of Gordon B. Hinckley,* 236.
7. *Teachings of the Prophet Joseph Smith,* 370.
8. Paulsen, "Early Christian Belief in a Corporeal Deity," 105–16; "Doctrine of Divine Embodiment," 7–94.
9. Smith, *Doctrines of Salvation,* 1:12; McConkie, *Promised Messiah,* 166.
10. Ballard, "Building Bridges of Understanding," 6–7.
11. Smith, *Gospel Doctrine,* 96.
12. McConkie, Conference Report, October 1973, 55–56.
13. First Presidency Preface, *Hymns,* ix.

CHAPTER 15

FEAR NOT

WHY DO WE SERVE? WHY do we go to church? Why do we live the Word of Wisdom? Why do we avoid R-rated movies and pornography? Why do we avoid immorality in every form? Many people in the Church are in good standing and thus qualify for a temple recommend. Why do they do what they do, and why do they avoid what they avoid? For many, the motivation to keep the commandments is fear—fear of rejection by friends or family, fear of being arrested or of contracting a life-threatening disease, fear of encountering disciplinary measures in the Church, and fear of having to face God one day.

To be sure, fear is not a bad motive. Sometimes there seems to be nothing except "harshness, preaching and prophesying of wars, and contentions, and destructions, and continually reminding [us] of death, and the duration of eternity, and the judgments and the power of God, and all these things—stirring [us] up continually to keep [us] in the fear of the Lord" (Enos 1:23). Yes, sometimes the prophets and apostles and Church leaders must resort to speaking of such consequences to sin as endless torment and eternal damnation so "that it might work upon the hearts of the children of men" (D&C 19:7). It is better to be afraid of sin and to be frightened of the effects of willful wandering than to sin or wander. Once in a while, we simply need to have the word of the Lord shake us in our boots to remind us why we are here, who we are, and whose we are. In that sense, fear serves a useful purpose in forewarning us and calling us to repentance.

If fear is our only motive for faithfulness, however, we will eventually become weary and beaten down spiritually, or we will begin to ignore the word of truth and turn a deaf ear to the invitation to change. Further, we will never come to know the Lord, trust the Lord, and enjoy a quiet confidence in the Lord unless we are motivated by other things.

Matthew 25 contains what might be called three parables of preparation: the parable of the ten virgins, the parable of the sheep and the goats, and the parable of the talents. They all say something about how to prepare for the second coming of the Son of Man and the time of judgment. The parable of the ten virgins speaks of the need for a consistent, ongoing program of spiritual growth and of the problem of trying to suddenly develop spirituality. The parable of the sheep and the goats teaches that those who are prepared to meet the Lord are those who have come to love and serve, those whose hearts are drawn out in compassion to the least of our brothers and sisters. And the parable of the talents teaches the need for industry and faithfulness in the Lord's kingdom.

Not long ago, while sitting in an inspiring Gospel Doctrine class, I saw something else in the parable of the talents I had never seen before. In this parable, as you know, the master travels to a far country and leaves differing talents—amounts of money, in this case—with three men. The master expects them to build upon what they have received, to be productive and industrious with what they have been given. When he returns, he praises and rewards the man whose five talents have been doubled, and he likewise praises and rewards the one whose two talents have also been doubled.

"Then he which had received the one talent came and said, Lord, I knew thee that thou art an hard man, reaping where thou hast not sown, and gathering where thou hast not strawed: and I was afraid, and went and hid thy talent in the earth: lo, there thou hast that is thine." The master was angry and responded: "Thou wicked and slothful servant, thou knewest that I reap where I sowed not, and gather where I have not strawed: thou oughtest therefore to have put my money to the exchangers, and then at my coming I should have received mine own with usury [interest]. Take therefore the talent from him, and give it unto him which hath ten talents. For unto every one that hath shall be given, and he shall have abundance: but from him that hath not shall be taken away even that which he hath. And cast ye the unprofitable servant into outer darkness: there shall be weeping and gnashing of teeth" (Matthew 25:14–30).

Generally when we speak of the meaning of this parable, we focus on the need for us to use our talents wisely—our gifts, abilities, or even financial resources—to become more profitable servants. We assume, I suppose rightly, that the master in this parable is God, that he has given to each one of us things we should enhance and improve in order to contribute to the building of the kingdom of God and the establishment of Zion, and that he will soon come again, at which point we will be required to stand before him and account for what we did with what he gave us. And perhaps this is just what the Savior wants us to understand from the parable of the talents.

There is a less obvious aspect of the parable which we may also find profitable to consider: the unproductive steward saw his master as hard or strict, one who punishes and condemns. I believe this perspective of the master—which is undoubtedly an ill-advised and inaccurate one—directly affected how the steward behaved. What we believe affects what we do. If we live our lives in constant fear of God—in dread or unhealthy fear—then our actions will seldom if ever spring from proper motives, such as love of God and a longing to serve our fellow-man. Rather, we will approach each day with the kind of fear and trembling that leads to fretful and unproductive living.

We know that our God has all power and that he can, as the scriptures attest, smite us with one glance of his all-searching eye. His is the power and the prerogative to give life and to take it. We are told that we should fear God and that the fear of the Lord is the beginning of wisdom (Psalm 111:10; Proverbs 1:7; 9:10). We are told that we should "work out [our] own salvation with fear and trembling" (Philippians 2:12). But almost always the word translated *fear* may also be translated as *reverence*. That is, we should honor and respect and reverence our God. He is the Man of Holiness (Moses 6:57), the God of all creation, the embodiment of every virtue and perfection. But he is also our Father in Heaven, the Father of our spirits, a kind and loving Parent who delights in our happiness and yearns to save us, one and all, with an everlasting salvation (D&C 43:25).

Although this may be taking liberties with the parable of the talents, I suggest that the Lord does indeed want us to be productive with what we have but that he in no way desires to compare us with others nor is the quantity of the return of any special interest to him. I believe that if one of the servants in the parable had sincerely worked and labored to improve upon his talent but had in the end been unable to expand appreciably upon the original amount, the Lord would have accepted his offering. Truly, "the Lord requireth the heart and a willing mind" (D&C 64:34). We are judged by the desires of our heart as well as by our works (Alma 41:3; D&C 137:9).

In speaking of a little-known person in our Church history, a man by the name of Oliver Granger—called to serve as the agent of the First Presidency in Kirtland while the Saints moved themselves to Missouri—the Lord said: "I remember my servant Oliver Granger; behold, verily I say unto him that his name shall be had in sacred remembrance from generation to generation, forever and ever, saith the Lord." And then these tender and consoling words, words that teach us a great deal about the Being we worship: "Therefore, let him contend earnestly for the redemption of the First Presidency of my Church, saith the Lord; and when he falls he shall rise again, for his sacrifice shall be more sacred unto me than his increase, saith the Lord" (D&C 117:12–13).

How we view the Lord affects how we live the gospel. If in every move we make we find ourselves looking over our shoulder to make certain that God isn't going to smite us should we fail or fall short, our offering will not be from the heart nor will the product of our labors be fruitful. And, frankly, it just wouldn't be much fun to choose the right. Who wants to live that way?

On the other hand, if we see our Heavenly Father and his Son Jesus Christ for who and what they are—glorified, exalted beings whose whole purpose is to "bring to pass the immortality and eternal life of man" (Moses 1:39) and whose greatest desire is for all of us to inherit exaltation—then our hearts will be lighter, our actions will be motivated by love and acceptance, and our work will be profitable and enjoyable.

Only in and through the Savior can we be changed and renewed, made clean and free from guilt and shame, relieved of the anxiety and unhealthy dread associated with fearful living. As we properly confess our sins and forsake them, the blood of Christ sanctifies us from worldliness and from a stilted view of things. The more pure we become—and this purity comes only through Christ, by the power of the Holy Ghost— the more clearly we are able to see things as they really are. When we continue in sin, we are unable to see things clearly; we see things as *we* are, not as *they* are in reality. But the power of the Atonement gives us a new heart and a new mind and new eyes with which to see things. We feel and think and perceive an entirely new realm of reality.

These blessings come to us through the mercy and love of the Lord Jesus Christ. But they do not come to us fully until we choose to repent, to turn away from our sins, and to be transformed in our minds and our hearts (Romans 12:1–3). In speaking of charity, or the pure love of Christ, Mormon implored, "Wherefore, my beloved brethren [and sisters], pray unto the Father with all the energy of heart, that ye may be filled with this love, which he hath bestowed upon all who are true followers of his Son, Jesus Christ; that ye may become the sons [and daughters] of God; that when he shall appear we shall be like him, for we shall see him as he is; that we may have this hope; that we may be purified even as he is pure" (Moroni 7:48).

Generally when we speak of charity, we speak of the love we should demonstrate toward our brothers and sisters. But let us be clear in our minds that we will never be in a position to love purely and have a meaningful effect on the lives of others until we have experienced the pure love of Christ in our own hearts and minds. Elder Jeffrey R. Holland wrote: "It is instructive to note that the charity or 'the pure love of Christ,' we are to cherish can be interpreted two ways. One of its meanings is the kind of merciful, forgiving love Christ's disciples should have one for another. That is, all Christians should try to love as the Savior loved, showing pure, redeeming compassion for all. Unfortunately, few, if any, mortals have been entirely successful in this endeavor, but it is an invitation that all should try to meet.

"The greater definition of 'the pure love of Christ,' however, is not what we as Christians try but largely fail to demonstrate toward others but rather what Christ totally succeeded in demonstrating toward us. True charity has been known only once. It is shown perfectly and purely in Christ's unfailing, ultimate, and atoning love for us. It is Christ's love for us that 'suffereth long, and is kind, and envieth not.' It is his love for us that is not 'puffed up . . . , not easily provoked, thinketh no evil.' It is Christ's love for us that 'beareth all things, believeth all things, hopeth all things, endureth all things.' It is as demonstrated in Christ that 'charity never faileth.' It is that charity—his pure love for us—without which we would be nothing, hopeless, of all men and women most miserable. Truly, those found possessed of the blessings of his love at the last day—the Atonement, the Resurrection, eternal life, eternal promise—surely it shall be well with them.

"This does not in any way," Elder Holland continues, "minimize the commandment that we are to try to acquire this kind of love for one another. We should 'pray unto the Father with all the energy of heart that [we] may be filled with this love.' We should try to be more constant and unfailing, more longsuffering and kind, less envious and puffed up in our relationships with others. As Christ lived so should we live, and as Christ loved so should we love. But the 'pure love of Christ' Mormon spoke of is precisely that—Christ's love. *With that divine gift, that redeeming bestowal, we have everything; without it we have nothing and ultimately are nothing,* except in the end 'devils [and] angels to a devil.'

"Life has its share of fears and failures. Sometimes things fall short. Sometimes people fail us, or economies or businesses or governments fail us. But one thing in time or eternity does not fail us—the pure love of Christ."[1]

The new life in Christ enables and empowers us to live peacefully, peaceably, and comfortably, even as hell rages on all sides. The revelations declare that "he that looketh on a woman to lust after her, or if any shall commit adultery in their hearts, they shall not have the Spirit, but shall deny the faith and shall fear" (D&C 63:16). On the other hand, those who "let virtue garnish [their] thoughts unceasingly" feel confidence "in the presence of God" (D&C 121:45). Fear. Confidence. Which do we want? Which of these appeals to us? Those who choose to live the gospel—to repent and submit to the will of the Lord, to deny themselves of all ungodliness (Moroni 10:32)—enjoy that quiet and sublime confidence, that peace which passes all understanding (Philippians 4:7). Truly, as John the Beloved wrote, "If our heart condemn us not, then have we confidence toward God" (1 John 3:21; compare 2:28; 5:14).

The Lord never intended for us to languish in guilt or to live in constant anxiety concerning whether we are pleasing a hard-to-please God. Each of us has within ourselves a manifestation of the Light of Christ or the Spirit of Jesus Christ (Moroni 7:16–19). It is our conscience, that inborn, inherent moral monitor that points us toward the right and warns us of the wrong. If we give heed to that light, we are led to higher light and knowledge (D&C 84:46–48) as well as a deeper measure of joy and fulfillment. If we ignore or spurn the warnings of the Light, we weaken our resistance to sin and distance ourselves from Deity. We then become oblivious to the Light and resentful of those who possess it. We fear, and we feel tension and anxiety, frustration and noise within our souls.

The Prophet Joseph Smith taught: "If you wish to go where God is, you must be like God, or possess the principles which God possesses, for if we are not drawing towards God in principle, we are going from Him and drawing towards the devil. . . .

"Search your hearts and see if you are like God. I have searched mine, and feel to repent of all my sins. . . .

"As far as we degenerate from God, we descend to the devil and lose knowledge, and without knowledge we cannot be saved, and while our hearts are filled with evil, and we are studying evil, there is no room in our hearts for good, or studying good. Is not God good? Then you be good; if He is faithful, then you be faithful."[2]

The gospel of Jesus Christ is in reality a gospel covenant. As a part of that covenant, we agree to do those things that we *can* do—to have faith, to repent, to be baptized and receive the gift of the Holy Ghost, and to endure faithfully to the end of our lives. For his part, the Lord agrees to do for us what we *cannot* do for ourselves—forgive our sins, cleanse and purify our hearts, empower us in our efforts to keep the commandments, raise us from the dead, and endow us with glory and honor hereafter. C. S. Lewis observed: "Christians have often disputed as to whether what leads the Christian home is good actions, or faith in Christ. . . . [I]t does seem to me like asking which blade in a pair of scissors is most necessary. . . . You see, we are now trying to understand, and to separate into watertight compartments, what exactly God does and what man does when God and man are working together."[3]

Perhaps the most well-known passage in LDS literature on this delicate balance is found in the Book of Mormon. "For we labor diligently," Nephi explained, "to write, to persuade our children, and also our brethren, to believe in Christ, and to be reconciled to God; for we know that it is by grace that we are saved, after all we can do" (2 Nephi 25:23; see also 10:24; Alma 24:10–11). That is, above and beyond all we can do, we are saved by the grace of Christ; salvation is still "the greatest of all the gifts of God" (D&C 6:13; 14:7). Further, the more we learn to trust the Lord and rely upon his merits and mercy, the less anxious we become about life here and hereafter.

Our Heavenly Father and his Son Jesus Christ are eager to do all in their power to welcome us back, to make us better and truer than we are now, and to bring into our lives the peace and assurance that we are on course. C. S. Lewis wrote further: "No amount of falls will really undo us if we keep on picking ourselves up each time. We shall of course be v[ery] muddy and tattered children by the time we reach home. But the bathrooms are all ready, the towels put out, and the clean clothes in the airing cupboard. The only fatal thing is to lose one's temper and give it up. It is when we notice the dirt that God is most present in us: it is the v[ery] sign of His presence."[4]

The story is told of a woman who visited President Joseph Fielding Smith. She had been guilty of serious transgression but had fully repented and now just wanted to find her way. President Smith asked her to read to him from Genesis the story of the destruction of Sodom and Gomorrah and of Lot's wife being turned to a pillar of salt. He asked her what lesson was to be learned. She answered, essentially, "The message of that story is that God will destroy the wicked." "Not so," President Smith told this repentant woman. "The message for you is: 'Don't look back!'"[5]

"Therefore, fear not, little flock; do good; let earth and hell combine against you, for if ye are built upon my rock, they cannot prevail. . . . Look unto me in every thought; doubt not, fear not " (D&C 6:34, 36). Truly, "if [we] are prepared [we] shall not fear" (D&C 38:30).

NOTES
1. Holland, *Christ and the New Covenant,* 336–37; italics added.
2. *Teachings of the Prophet Joseph Smith,* 216–17.
3. Lewis, *Mere Christianity,* 131–32.
4. *Letters of C. S. Lewis,* 365.
5. Cited in Packer, "Fountain of Life," 11.

CHAPTER 16

DESCENDING INTO GLORY

O NE OF THE REALITIES OF Christian discipleship is that a person must descend in order to rise. That is, the path to glory is a downward path, a route that leads necessarily through pain and heartache and irony. After having transgressed in Eden, Adam and Eve were forbidden to partake of the fruit of the tree of life. They were required to pass through mortality before they would be prepared for immortality, to descend to the depths before they could participate in the majesty of celestial life. And so it is with all of us.

Nephi was given a vision of the condescension of God (1 Nephi 11). Having seen first how the Almighty Elohim would join with a mortal woman to bring forth a son, the Only Begotten Son of God, he witnessed the condescension of God the Son—the coming to earth of Jehovah, the descent into mortality of the Lord Omnipotent. Indeed, the son of Lehi was taught a powerful message—that only through condescension could the consummation of the great plan of happiness be brought to pass. The God of our fathers was required to descend below all things in order to be able to ascend to celestial heights, and, moreover, for the sons and daughters of Adam and Eve to do the same.

The apostle Paul described Christ's descent below all things: "Let this mind be in you, which was also in Christ Jesus: who, being in the form of God, thought it not robbery to be equal with God: but made himself of no reputation, and took upon him the form of a servant, and was made in the likeness of men: and being found in fashion as a man, he humbled himself, and became obedient unto death, even the death of the cross. Wherefore," Paul continued, "God also hath highly exalted him, and given him a name which is above every name" (Philippians 2:5–9). As Paul said elsewhere, "Ye know the grace of our Lord Jesus Christ, that, though he was rich, yet for your sakes he became poor, that ye through his poverty might be rich" (2 Corinthians 8:9). Also, "he that descended ["into the lower parts of the earth"; Ephesians 4:9] is the same also that ascended up far above all heavens, that he might fill all things" (Ephesians 4:10).

Jesus was spared no agony. There was no pain, no suffering, no loneliness or alienation, no bitter draught he was not required to imbibe. In Gethsemane and on Golgotha, he truly descended below all things that he might comprehend all things (D&C 88:6), that thereby his empathy for all men and women might be perfected (Alma 7:11–13). Jesus trod the winepress alone and was thus subject to "the fierceness of the wrath of Almighty God" (Isaiah 63:3; D&C 76:107; 88:106; 133:50), the withdrawal of the Father's strengthening Spirit. He suffered more than man—meaning mortal man, unaided by divine influence—can suffer (Mosiah 3:7). Truly, as Joseph Smith explained, Jesus Christ "descended in suffering below that which man can suffer; or, in other words, suffered greater sufferings, and was exposed to more powerful contradictions than any man can be."[1]

Two Christian writers observed: "Once His life on earth began, Jesus never stopped descending. Omnipotent, He cried; the owner of all things, He had no home. The King of Kings, He became a bondservant; the source of truth, He was found guilty of blasphemy; the Creator, He was spit on by the creatures; the giver of life, He was crucified naked on a cross—bleeding, gasping for air. With His death, the descent was complete—from the pinnacle of praise in the universe to the ultimate debasement and torture of death on a cross, the innocent victim of human wickedness."[2]

And what of this suffering and death? What of this condescension? We know it was necessary in order for the infinite atoning sacrifice to be accomplished. But is there more? Is such a thing expected of us? Of course we are in no position to suffer and bleed and die for others' sins and infirmities. Of course we cannot die and raise ourselves from the tomb and thereby open the door to immortality, as did our Master. Jesus is the only Savior of mankind. But is there a pattern, a type, in his condescension that has direct application to our lives?

The call of Christ is a call to be downwardly mobile. This is "not just a matter of how much money we give away, but how much of ourselves we yield, how much of the sin and excess in our lives we are willing to tear away. It is an attitude marked by strength of character. And we do not grow in character without pain."[3] The challenge to live in the world without being of the world is the challenge of seeing to it that our attachments, our values, and our loyalties are not determined or driven by telestial things. The fleeting and the ephemeral must not obsess us. In reality, it is not the case that the one who leaves this world with the most toys wins in the game of life. The Christan call to downward mobility is not necessarily the call to failure or obscurity, but our covenant with Christ must be secure enough in our souls that we would be willing to be judged a failure by this world's standards or to be excluded from the chief seats in the secular synagogues if faithfulness to principle required it. Truly, down is the only way up.

We live in a world where winning is everything. There are few rewards in our society for second place. We are taught from childhood the absolute necessity of excelling, of being the best in the class, the finest on the block, the most successful in the industry. Too often there develops in time within the will of the achiever a competitive spirit that can drive out cooperation, consideration, and compassion. Product becomes more prized than process and eventually more sacred than people. The world beckons us to seek for power. Christ calls upon us to yield. "Let's be honest. Doesn't the world's way make more sense? . . . If we gather enough power, we need rely only on ourselves. Trust becomes a matter of the size of our biceps or our B2s, or whatever else we use to measure strength. We can place our faith in a seen plan, and keep control.

"The way of Jesus seems, in comparison, almost ludicrous. If we yield power to others, we can no longer trust in ourselves. Trust becomes suddenly a matter of the size of our God. We must place our faith in an unseen hand, and divest ourselves of all semblance of control."[4]

The Savior calls us to lose—to lose ourselves in his work, to forsake notoriety or praise in the accomplishment of his purposes. He does not ask that we do less than our best or that we perform less than is required to do the job. What he does ask is that we be less concerned with what others think, less troubled by mortal pecking orders, less bothered by appearances than we are with reality. In the work of the ministry, we will be successful in the rescue of wandering sheep only to the degree that we care more about the sheep than with how we look, how we come across, how many sheep we rescue, or how our achievements are publicly acknowledged.

The disciple loses his life when he serves his fellowman, when he places others' comfort and convenience before his own. Our Exemplar said, "I am among you as he that serveth" (Luke 22:27). Service sanctifies both giver and receiver. Those who involve themselves in the work of the Master receive the approbation of the Master. As the Unassuming One announced: "Break not my commandments for to save your lives; for whosoever will save his life in this world, shall lose it in the world to come. And whosoever will lose his life in this world, for my sake, shall find it in the world to come. Therefore, forsake the world, and save your souls" (JST Matthew 16:27–29).

Losing ourselves entails more than being busily engaged in serving others, as essential as that is. It also involves putting off the natural man and putting on Christ. It is the natural man that seeks acclaim, that requires attention, that elicits compliments. "The natural life in each of us," C. S. Lewis wrote, "is something self-centred, something that wants to be petted and admired. . . . And especially it wants to be left to itself: to keep well away from anything better or stronger or higher than it, anything that might make it feel small. It is afraid of the light and air of the spiritual world, just as people who have been brought up to be dirty are afraid of a bath. And in a sense it is quite right. It knows that if the spiritual life gets hold of it, all its self-centredness and self-will are going to be killed and it is ready to fight tooth and nail to avoid that."[5] We thus lose ourselves when we find Christ, the Captain of our soul. We lose ourselves when we become less concerned with personal whims, more directed toward divine design. We lose ourselves when we are willing, without let or hindrance, to dedicate ourselves to The Church of Jesus Christ and labor with fidelity to assist in the establishment of the kingdom of God on earth.

The Lord calls us to lose—to lose our self-will, our self-promotion, our selfish desires—in favor of a greater and more far-reaching will. He calls us to have an eye single to his glory, to do things his way. Duplicity leads to darkness, while singleness leads to light. "And if your eye be single to my glory, your whole bodies shall be filled with light, and there shall be no darkness in you; and that body which is filled with light comprehendeth all things" (D&C 88:67). The Saints are forevermore sanctified and made holy through yielding their hearts unto God (Helaman 3:35). "When we put God first," President Ezra Taft Benson pointed out, "all other things fall into their proper place or drop out of our lives. Our love of the Lord will govern the claims for our affection, the demands on our time, the interests we pursue, and the order of our priorities."[6]

One sad commentary of this modern age is that so many have lost their way—the way to happiness, the way to peace, the way to genuine fulfillment. It just may be that those who work hardest at trying to find themselves, at least according to this world's standards and methods, will, unfortunately, continue to wander in the morass of existential anguish. Those who turn to the Lord and enter into covenant with him find themselves and make their way along the strait and narrow path that leads to the abundant life. That life is worth whatever paltry price we have to pay along the way, and in the end we shall see that there really was no sacrifice at all.

The call to lose is also a call to cooperate. Whereas the worldly seek to put down others through lifting themselves, the Saints are called upon to lift and build and strengthen their brothers and sisters. Whereas too often those driven by the competitive urge seek to abase others through exalting themselves, the Lord directs otherwise. Zion is built upon the principle of cooperation. The people of Zion labor for Zion, "that every man may improve upon his talent, that every man may gain other talents, yea, even an hundred fold . . . every man seeking the interest of his neighbor, and doing all things with an eye single to the glory of God" (D&C 82:18–19). The people of God find no pleasure in defeating others. There is no joy in winning for winning's sake. Rather, there is consummate joy in succoring the weak, lifting up the hands that hang down, and strengthening the feeble knees (D&C 81:5).

One day things will change. The lowly will be exalted. Unpretentious and spontaneously (but silent) righteous men and women will be acknowledged from the housetops. Malice and malevolence will melt away as the hoar frost, while benevolence and beneficence will become the order of the day. President Howard W. Hunter testified: "In a world too preoccupied with winning through intimidation and seeking to be number one, no large crowd of folk is standing in line to buy books that call for mere meekness. But the meek shall inherit the earth, a pretty impressive corporate takeover—and done without intimidation! Sooner or later—and we pray sooner rather than later—everyone will acknowledge that Christ's way is not only the *right* way, but ultimately the *only* way to hope and joy. Every knee shall bow and every tongue will confess that gentleness is better than brutality, that kindness is greater than coercion, that the soft voice turneth away wrath. In the end, and sooner than that whenever possible, we must be more like him."[7]

Babylon stresses acquisition. Zion calls its municipals to consecration. The Lord doesn't ask for much—he merely wants all of us! The Savior's warning against taking no thought for the morrow, what we shall wear or eat (Matthew 6:25; 3 Nephi 13:25), is actually a warning against undue anxiety regarding this world's goods and services. The Lord does not want his followers to starve or be undernourished. Nor does he desire that we be unbecoming in appearance or poorly attired. Rather, he calls us to do the right thing for the right reason, to eat to live, and to clothe our bodies that we might be protected from the elements. We need not kneel at the shrines of wooden or stone gods to be idolatrous. We need not offer sacrifice to a lifeless deity to have forsaken the faith of our fathers. Rather, we need only devote our time, talents, and means to the establishment or proliferation of a cause other than the gospel cause. False objects of adoration and worship in our day take the form of real estate or portfolios or chrome or furniture or leisure, none of which is innately evil but which as ends in themselves— rather than means—consume and corrupt. Any time things take precedence over persons, particularly the Person of Christ, we are on a downward spiral of personal apostasy. We have wandered off the path of the disciple.

There came to Jesus on one occasion a young man who sought the blessings of eternal life. He inquired about what was expected of him to achieve that glorious end. The Lord specified several of the Ten Commandments, to which the young man responded: "All these have I observed from my youth."

Mark adds tenderly: "Then Jesus beholding him loved him"—
for the fellow was a good man, a faithful man—"and said unto
him, One thing thou lackest: go thy way, sell whatsoever thou
hast, and give to the poor, and thou shalt have treasure in
heaven: and come, take up the cross, and follow me." Then
came the moment of truth: "And he [the young man] was sad
at that saying, and went away grieved: for he had great possessions" (Mark 10:17–22).

Is it necessary to give everything away in order to follow
Christ? In answer, we state simply that despite the fact that the
Church can always use the financial resources of its members
to assist in the spreading of the Lord's work throughout the
world, the matter of giving up or consecrating one's earthly
properties—literally, doing what we do "with sacredness"—is
of monumental importance in the formation of a disciple and
thus in becoming holy. It strikes at the heart of what it means to
come unto Christ. To take the yoke of Christ upon us, we must
remove the yoke of the world. To put on Christ, we must put
off the trappings and tinsel of this world.

Jesus said what he meant and meant what he said when he
taught that it is easier for a camel to go through the eye of a
needle than for a rich man who trusts in his riches to enter into
the kingdom of heaven (JST Matthew 19:26; compare JST
Mark 10:22–26; JST Luke 18:27). There is no metaphor
intended. No softening of this hard saying is justifiable. The
issue is one of trust. Reliance. Dependence. The Almighty, who
promises us all that he has, asks simply that we be willing to
give him all. Nothing else will do. "We are not always called
upon to live the whole law of consecration and give all of our
time, talents, and means to the building up of the Lord's earthly
kingdom," Elder Bruce R. McConkie taught. "Few of us are

called upon to sacrifice much of what we possess, and at the moment there is only an occasional martyr in the cause of revealed religion.

"But what the scriptural account means is that to gain celestial salvation we must be able to live these laws to the full if we are called upon to do so. Implicit in this is the reality that we must in fact live them to the extent we are called upon so to do."[8]

It is not that the Lord does not want his people to prosper. In fact, as Dietrich Bonhoeffer observed, "it is not important that I should have no possessions, but if I do I must keep them as though I had them not; in other words I must cultivate a spirit of inward detachment, so that my heart is not in my possessions."[9]

The anxiety that we mentioned earlier, an anxiety against which the Savior warned his disciples (Matthew 6:25; 3 Nephi 13:25) is concerned with future times, with *my* goods, *my* holdings, *my* ability to provide adequately. Truly, "the way to misuse our possessions is to use them as an insurance against the morrow. Anxiety is always directed to the morrow, whereas goods are in the strictest sense meant to be used only for today. By trying to ensure for the next day we are only creating uncertainty today. . . . The only way to win assurance is by leaving to-morrow entirely in the hands of God and by receiving from him all we need for today."[10]

The heavens proclaim that "the earth is the Lord's, and the fulness thereof; the world, and they that dwell therein" (Psalm 24:1). In a modern revelation, the Lord declared: "Behold, all these properties are mine, or else your faith is vain, and ye are found hypocrites, and the covenants which ye have made unto me are broken; and if the properties are mine, then ye are stewards; otherwise ye are no stewards" (D&C 104:55–56). All things belong to God. He created them, and he sustains and upholds them. A vital realization on the part of the man or woman who commits to follow the Redeemer is that he or she owns nothing but is a steward over God's properties. The Christian's descent into glory entails an awareness of our nothingness without Deity. King Benjamin thus explained to his people: "I say unto you, my brethren, that if you should render all the thanks and praise which your whole soul has power to possess, to that God who has created you, and has kept and preserved you, . . . I say unto you that if ye should serve him who has created you from the beginning, and is preserving you from day to day, by lending you breath, that ye may live and move and do according to your own will, and even supporting you from one moment to another—I say, if ye should serve him with all your whole souls yet ye would be unprofitable servants" (Mosiah 2:20–21).

Truly, as Joseph Smith taught in the School of the Prophets, a religion that does not require the sacrifice of all things does not have the power to produce the kind of saving faith in its members that will lead unto life and salvation.[11] Only when the people of the Lord are willing to give their all to the cause of truth—including their own lives, if necessary—do they place themselves in a position to lay hold on the blessings of eternal life. No one wants to die, even to die the death of a martyr. And yet how else could the Lord obtain that unconditional dedication from his people so necessary to the perpetuation of a system of salvation that spans the veil? Only a church that asks *everything* from its congregants can promise them, in the name of the Lord, everything in eternity.

The call of Christ is a call to humility. "Humble yourselves in the sight of the Lord," James wrote, "and he shall lift you up" (James 4:10). The Christian's descent into glory comes through the surrender of power, through self-abandonment, through servanthood, through sacrifice, and through the ready acknowledgment that without the renovating and transforming grace of the Messiah we are nothing. In this descent, as in all worthy endeavors, Jesus Christ is our Exemplar. "With his life and death as a man, Christ violated every tenet of the world's system. The Highest came to serve the lowest. The Creator and Sustainer of all things came to pour Himself out. The One who possessed everything became nothing. From the world's perspective, the cross became the symbol of foolishness. Yet in God's eyes, Christ became the greatest of the great. . . . And . . . because of Christ's downward mobility, God highly exalted Him, and gave Him a name above every name. That's the twist. Jesus Christ descended into God's greatness."[12]

NOTES

1. Smith, *Lectures on Faith*, 5:2; compare Hebrews 12:3.
2. Hybels and Wilkins, *Descending into Greatness*, 18–19.
3. Hybels and Wilkins, *Descending into Greatness*, 66.
4. Hybels and Wilkins, *Descending into Greatness*, 33.
5. Lewis, *Mere Christianity*, 155–56.
6. Benson, Conference Report, April 1988, 3.
7. Hunter, Conference Report, April 1993, 80; italics in original.
8. McConkie, Conference Report, April 1975, 74–75.
9. Bonhoeffer, *Cost of Discipleship*, 88.
10. Bonhoeffer, *Cost of Discipleship*, 197–98.
11. Smith, *Lectures on Faith*, 6:7.
12. Hybels and Wilkins, *Descending into Greatness*, 19.

CHAPTER 17

FRUITS OF HOLINESS

C HRISTIANS AROUND THE globe may disagree about whether Jesus of Nazareth was born of a virgin, healed the sick and raised the dead, died and rose again from the tomb. They may debate whether he was indeed God. But most agree—at least those who accept the accounts of his life and ministry in the Gospels—that he loved people, that he was the embodiment of compassion and empathy. Jesus loved. He was in the business of people.

Our Lord warned that in a day when iniquity would abound, the love of many would wax cold (D&C 45:27; Joseph Smith–Matthew 1:10, 30). Love is a priceless virtue, a heavenly quality, but it can survive only in the heart of one who is attempting to be true to what he or she knows to be right. To sin against light is to open the door to darkness and to close the door on those divine refinements that make men and women men and women of God. We can begin to understand why Alma counseled Shiblon: "See that ye bridle all your passions, that ye may be filled with love" (Alma 38:12). Truly,

"God is love; and he that dwelleth in love dwelleth in God, and God in him" (1 John 4:16). Lust leads to loneliness. Unbridled passions are followed by fear. "He that looketh on a woman to lust after her, or if any shall commit adultery in their hearts, they shall not have the Spirit, but shall deny the faith and shall fear" (D&C 63:16). Fear. Fear of being found out, fear of rejection, fear of coming face to face with the vainness of one's own life. On the other hand, one filled with the love of Christ does not waste his life in worry or ache with anxiety concerning the future. The love of Christ brings peace and contentment. It settles the soul, rests the road-weary, and consoles the bereaved. As John taught, "There is no fear in love; but perfect love casteth out fear" (1 John 4:18; compare Moroni 8:16).

A sad commentary of our time is the manner in which the refusal to abide by the divine standards of morality has led to so much unhappiness and abuse. Such doings testify that the love of God, given as a free gift through his Son Jesus Christ, has begun to wax cold and thus to wane in the hearts of earth's pilgrims. Wickedness weakens love. Surely if godlike love is a heavenly endowment, then reveling in sin prevents one from receiving and extending such love. Sexual immorality, for example, prostitutes those God-given powers that are so intimately connected with the fountains of human life. Lust is a pitiful substitute for that love which is pure, that expression and that commitment which bind and seal through time and eternity.

Although ours is not a moral society, it is possible to live a moral life in the midst of great sin. It is a challenge, to be sure, but it is possible. God has called upon those of us in the household of faith to stand aloof from the sins of this world. We do so as we avoid, as we would a plague (for surely it is), the pornography, the videos, the motion pictures, the television programs, the music, and the literature that stifle spiritual sensitivity and deaden those holy emotions and attributes that have always characterized the Lord's people. We are called to a life of holiness. We are called to be a light to a world that wanders in darkness.

Members of The Church of Jesus Christ of Latter-day Saints, those who have received the gift of the Holy Ghost, are entitled to that purifying and sanctifying influence that heightens our perspective on life and deepens our love for God and his children. Surely people who know where they come from, why they are here, and where they are going can view the world and its inhabitants with a compassion and a concern that few others can fathom; surely those who have by covenant come out of the world unto Christ can seek for and eventually embody that love and gentility of soul that are central to the nature of our Master. Ours is a great opportunity to be a leavening influence in the earth, to become as oil on troubled waters. Like salt, however, our influence is direct and lasting only to the degree that we have not lost our savor through mixture and contamination. The love of the Lord can shine through us to a lonely and unhappy world only as we have allowed ourselves to become pure receptacles.

If I were totally honest, I would admit that twenty years ago talks about love in church basically turned me off. I thought it was a rather mushy subject, a topic that was sweet, to be sure, but one that was less than worthy of the time of the Saints. Why, I reasoned, we might as well talk about flowers or sunsets or lovely landscapes. It was sort of a given in my mind that people ought to love one another, and so love seemed something that ought to be confined to the slogans or pep talks of the Rotary Club. Doctrine was what I demanded; theology was my thing. Well, I still love to discuss the doctrines of the gospel and find great joy in doing so. I still believe the time in the sacred meetings of the Church is precious and should only be taken up in substantive matters, in saving truths worthy of the blood of Jesus Christ and the death of Joseph Smith. But a few things have changed in my life, things that tend now to focus my attention not only on God's revelations but also on his ultimate creation—his children.

I have met many noble sons and daughters of God, many people who may not be able to explain the intricacies of the Atonement but who nonetheless have the image of Christ in their countenances. I have become acquainted with men and women who constitute that vast body of souls we know as the rank and file of the Church, who by divine standards embody gospel greatness. Many of these choice individuals have lived lives of quiet goodness. Their righteousness is unpretentious, their service spontaneous, unpremeditated, and silent. They love as the Lord loves. They are not immune from life's challenges. They agonize over children who stray. They wrestle with personal weaknesses. But they love as the Lord loves. Their lives bring to mind the story told by Luke of a woman—a sinner by some persons' self-righteous standards—who washed Jesus' feet with her tears, anointed them with ointment, and then wiped them with her hair. Responding to the thoughts of those who prejudged her and were incensed that the Master would allow such an one to minister to him, Jesus said: "Her sins, which are many, are forgiven; for she loved much: but to whom little is forgiven, the same loveth little. And he said unto her, Thy sins are forgiven. . . . Thy faith hath saved thee; go in peace" (Luke 7:47–48, 50).

As my own soul has been wrenched and stretched by the painful strugglings of this life; as I have wept and prayed and sorrowed for my own sins and those of my loved ones; as my hardened heart has been broken and my spirit crushed under the weight of some of the ironies of this existence, I have come to appreciate with certainty that some things really matter. I have come to believe that feelings are fundamental, that people matter more than anything, that people's feelings are sacred. I have a witness that God expects me to be gentle to his little ones, whether infant or aged. He expects us all to be kind.

Some years ago Elder Jeffrey R. Holland, then president of Brigham Young University, said something about the marriage relationship that went straight to the core of my being. I knew then that it was true and that I was under obligation to conform to its implications. The message reaches well beyond the attitudes and actions of husbands and wives. "To give ourselves so totally to another person," Elder Holland observed, "is the most trusting and perhaps the most fateful step we take in life. It seems such a risk and such an act of faith. None of us moving toward the altar would seem to have the confidence to reveal everything that we are—all our hopes, all our fears, all our dreams, all our weaknesses—to another person. Safety and good sense and this world's experience suggest that we hang back a little, that we not wear our heart on our sleeve where it can so easily be hurt by one who knows so much about us. We fear, as Zechariah prophesied of Christ, that we will be 'wounded in the house of [our] friends.' (Zechariah 13:6.)

" . . . Pat and I have lived together for [many] years. . . . I may not know everything about her, but I know [many] years' worth, and she knows that much of me. I know her likes and dislikes, and she knows mine. I know her tastes and interests and hopes and dreams, and she knows mine. As our love has grown and our relationship matured, we have been increasingly open with each other about all of that for [those] years now, and the result is that I know much more clearly how to help her and I know exactly how to hurt her. I may not know all the buttons to push, but I know most of them. And surely God will hold me accountable for any pain I cause her by intentionally pushing the hurtful ones when she has been so trusting of me. To toy with such a sacred trust—her body, her spirit, and her eternal future—and exploit those for my gain, even if only emotional gain, should disqualify me to be her husband and ought to consign my miserable soul to hell. To be that selfish would mean that I am a legal, live-in roommate who shares her company but I am not her husband in any Christian sense of that word. I have not been as Christ is to the church."[1]

It may be that the Keeper of the gate will not be as interested in how much we know at the great day of judgment or how busy we have been as in what we have become. Our mortal medals and our temporal acquisitions may prove to be far less significant in the eternal scheme of things than the enduring personal relationships we have developed and nurtured. Holy writ attests that the depth of our conversion is reflected in the way we view and treat one another. The apostle John wrote, "Beloved, let us love one another: for love is of God; and every one that loveth is born of God, and knoweth God" (1 John 4:7). Elder Marvin J. Ashton pointed out: "The way we treat each other is the foundation of the gospel of Jesus Christ." Further, "When we truly become converted to Jesus Christ, committed to Him, an interesting thing happens: our attention turns to the welfare of our fellowmen, and the way we treat others becomes increasingly filled with patience, kindness, a gentle acceptance, and a desire to play a positive role in their lives. This is the beginning of true conversion."[2]

The gifts of the Spirit are discussed at length by the apostle Paul (1 Corinthians 12–14), Moroni (Moroni 10), and the Lord in a revelation to the Prophet Joseph Smith (D&C 46). These gifts are one of the signs of the true Church, one of the evidences that God is indeed working through and with a people. Spiritual gifts are the signs and wonders and miracles that are always found among the Lord's covenant people. Such gifts as testimony, discernment, revelation, prophecy, tongues, teaching, wisdom, knowledge, healing, administration, and many others—these are like parts of the human body or the body of Christ, the Church (see 1 Corinthians 12). The Church provides a gathering place for individuals to share their gifts. Every member of the Church has at least one spiritual gift (D&C 46:11), and participation in the Church allows us to draw upon those various gifts and graces. Brother Jones may have the gift of healing, Sister Backman the gift of wisdom, Brother Brown the gift of teaching, and Sister Young the gift of discernment.

Though we must strive to be worthy of such gifts, there is a sense in which they come to us almost in spite of ourselves: because the Lord desires to bless the people of the covenant, he works his mysterious wonders through fallible, mortal creatures. To be more specific, let us suppose that in a given ward Brother Brown has the gift of teaching. The Lord has blessed this man with unusual insight into scripture and a capacity to expound upon those insights and involve the members of the Church profitably in the discovery of the sacred truths of the gospel. People love to hear him speak and teach. He proves a rich blessing to the Saints. And yet we find, on closer inspection, that this particular brother has difficulty with his temper, tends to explode over relatively insignificant matters, and can be downright harsh and insensitive when it comes to people's feelings.

We all rejoice in his gift, a gift that blesses others. We do not expect Brother Brown to be perfect, even though we certainly wish he were kinder and more Christlike in his dealings with people. No doubt there are some things Brother Brown does that please the Lord, and his relative worthiness allows him to possess this gift. And yet it would be unfortunate if Brother Brown were to conclude that his gift of teaching— which all who know him acknowledge to be his gift—were a sign of God's ready acceptance of his life, that his life was totally on track. The scriptures speak of how to know we are growing spiritually, how to know whether or not we are becoming a holy people.

We appropriate Christ's strength through the power of the Holy Ghost. When that Spirit dwells in us, we begin to bear the "fruit of the Spirit." Paul contrasts the "works of the flesh"— such things as adultery, fornication, idolatry, witchcraft, hatred, strife, and so forth, behaviors and attitudes characterizing the natural man—with the fruit of the Spirit, those works and dispositions that characterize the man or woman who has been born again. "The fruit of the Spirit is love, joy, peace, long-suffering, gentleness, goodness, faith, meekness, temperance. . . . And they that are Christ's have crucified the flesh with the affections and lusts." Paul then offers this wonderful plea to the household of faith: "If we live in the Spirit, let us also walk in the Spirit" (Galatians 5:19, 22–25).

Stated differently, if we claim membership in The Church of Jesus Christ, let's act like it. If we profess discipleship, people who observe us ought to be able to discern that discipleship without great difficulty. In today's jargon, if we talk the talk, we really ought to walk the walk! The fruits of the Spirit are those characteristics and attributes that flow from a changed heart, the ways that truly Christlike people feel and act. It's a wonderful thing to be a gospel scholar, to be learned in our theology; it's even more of a blessing to know our doctrine and also to embody pure religion (James 1:27). It's a privilege to possess the gift of healing, to be able to lay hands on the sick and, acting for and in behalf of the Lord, witness their recovery; it's a treasure beyond price to be able to love others after the manner of our Master and witness the healing power of that love.

I am haunted by the Savior's warnings against self-righteousness every time I read the four Gospels. Again and again he attacks the craft of those who profit from others' weakness and poverty, and he chides those who are scrupulous in their observance of ritual but heartless and unforgiving toward those who fall short. It has been rightly observed that "the more unsavory the characters, the more at ease they seemed to feel around Jesus. People like these found Jesus appealing: a Samaritan social outcast, a military officer of the tyrant Herod, a quisling tax collector, a recent hostess to seven demons.

"In contrast, Jesus got a chilly response from more respectable types. Pious Pharisees thought him uncouth and worldly, a rich young ruler walked away shaking his head, and even the open-minded Nicodemus sought a meeting under the cover of darkness." Then this chilling observation: "Somehow we have created a community of respectability in the church. . . . The down-and-out, who flocked to Jesus when he lived on earth, no longer feel welcome. How did Jesus, the only perfect person in history, manage to attract the notoriously imperfect? And what keeps us from following in his steps today?"[3]

The Prophet Joseph Smith taught: "Christ said he came to call sinners to repentance, to save them. Christ was condemned by the self-righteous Jews because He took sinners into his society; He took them upon the principle that they repented of their sins. . . .

"It is one evidence that men are unacquainted with the principles of godliness to behold the contraction of affectionate feelings and lack of charity in the world. The power and glory of godliness is spread out on a broad principle to throw out the mantle of charity. God does not look on sin with allowance, but when men have sinned, there must be allowance made for them.

"All the religious world is boasting of righteousness: it is the doctrine of the devil to retard the human mind, and hinder our progress, by filling us with self-righteousness. The nearer we get to our heavenly Father, the more we are disposed to look with compassion on perishing souls; we feel that we want to take them upon our shoulders, and cast their sins behind our backs." The Prophet added this directive: "You must repent, and get the love of God. Away with self-righteousness!"[4]

One way we know we are growing up spiritually, maturing in the qualities of holiness, and preparing ourselves to be with our Maker is the extent to which we become more and more sensitive to people—to their plights, to their challenges, to their silent strugglings. Sometimes I have been surprised at how insensitive we can be to one another when, in fact, we had no intention of being unkind but simply didn't think before we spoke. It is not uncommon, for example, for members of the

Church to inquire about personal and private matters, to go where wisdom and good judgment would never lead us. For example, when our sixth child was about three years old, a sister in the ward asked me, "How many children do you have now?" I answered that Stephen was our sixth.

"How many do you plan to have?" she followed up.

"I don't know," I answered. "That's up to the Lord."

Then the woman went further. "Well, when do you plan to have your next one?"

I was absolutely stunned by her blatant insensitivity, her utter inability to know that she was inquiring into areas that were none of her business. I responded with something like this: "You know, I'm not sure yet, but I can see that this is a very real concern to you. Once Shauna and I have had a chance to talk it through, we'll get back with you."

This episode merely points up an example of a person who was devoid of the social graces (and of judgment) to know when to keep quiet. There was really no harm done. Too often, however, people's feelings are injured and their sense of worth is seriously challenged by ill-advised comments or inappropriate questions. For a number of years when I was young, my family was not active in the Church. We attended church off and on, and my only continuing contact was a caring Primary teacher who picked me up every Thursday afternoon without fail. When a small branch of the Church was organized in a city several miles from where I grew up, my family was asked to attend there. I suppose my dad felt that it was time to get into gear spiritually and, maybe sensing that a new beginning would be the best thing, we started back to church.

The first Sunday when we returned home from Sunday School (those were the days when we had both morning and evening meetings), I overheard my father share some tender feelings with my mother. Dad explained that someone had come up to him at church and said, "Well, my goodness! What do we have here? You mean *you* decided to come to church? I think the walls are going to fall down!"

Through his tears I heard my remarkable father utter these words, words that I will never forget, words that are emblazoned upon my soul: "This is my church too. No man is going to run me out of my church."

Dad was soon called to serve as a counselor in the presidency of the Young Men's Mutual Improvement Association, then as a counselor in the branch presidency, and eventually as the first bishop of the ward. He was later called to serve as a counselor in the stake presidency in the newly created stake in that area.

I will be forever grateful that Dad had the courage of his convictions and that he did not allow another's insensitivity and coarseness to deter him. But I wonder why anyone would not have the decency to think through the implications (and effect) of such comments. "Aren't you ever going to get married?" is a question that is asked much, much too often of single members of the Church, especially women who would desperately love to begin their own family but have no control over their present circumstances. Similar comments are made to those who are divorced, those who are widowed, those who choose not to serve full-time missions but who want to be fully involved in the Church, those who are disadvantaged in some way—all comments that need never be made. One of the signs of a Christlike nature is that our hearts reach out in love to our brothers and sisters, and our words build and inspire and strengthen others.

To love and be loved is a glorious thing, especially in a world where in recent years men's and women's hearts have grown cold. I have come to know that the love of God—what the scriptures denominate as charity, the pure love of Christ (Moroni 7:47)—is not of this world. It is not man-made, and it cannot be manufactured. It is not something that can be programmed. It is of God. It is bestowed by him. I have had a few experiences with this divine principle that attest to its power and influence for good. I share a couple of them here, hoping that what I have learned may be of benefit.

As a new seminary instructor, I was assigned to teach the Old Testament to six classes of ninth graders. Having grown up in Louisiana, I had never had the opportunity to attend seminary or institute programs, and so I was ignorant about what this new experience would entail. As I lay in bed at night during the weeks before school started, I had marvelous visions of what lay ahead. I could picture myself walking into the classroom, Wilford Woodruff-like, teaching and expounding with great power, watching as young hearts and minds exploded with new insights as well as feelings of testimony and conversion.

To say that this was not exactly the experience I did have would be the grossest of understatements. It was awful. Those kids could not have cared less about what I knew. I quit every afternoon, only to have my principal and my wife bind up my wounds, paste me back together, and send me into the arena the next morning. Each night my prayers went something like this: "Heavenly Father, please bless these irreverent and irresponsible little creatures that they will sense that what I have to say is important. Help them want to be quiet and listen to my lessons."

There was something, however, about the pounding I was taking each day that began to humble me and force me to pray with greater intensity and deeper earnestness. One night, when I was simply up against the wall, naked in my inabilities and shorn of duplicity and pride, I found myself praying something like the following: "O Lord, thy servants the prophets have told us that these young people are precious in thy sight and that they have been reserved to come to earth in the Saturday night of time, in a day of great challenge and wickedness. I feel greatly inadequate to accomplish what needs to be done. They need to be prepared, to be taught the gospel. But I am weak and frail, and my feelings for them are not as they should be. Forgive me. Purify my heart and my affections. Make me worthy to teach the youth of the Church."

I do not remember feeling anything unusual at that moment except the sweet peace that comes when we have offered our all to the Lord and presented our petitions to him in sincerity. I walked into my first class the next morning prepared for the typical struggle. The devotional was presented, and the prayer was said. I remember very well sitting atop one of the desks and looking out at the class. And then something happened—something totally unexpected. I no longer saw these young people in the same way. As I looked into their eyes, there came into my heart an overwhelming feeling of love, a desire to reach out and lift and embrace each one of them. For some moments I was unable to speak, only to look at them and feel what I felt. The first words I spoke were these: "I wish I could tell you what I feel."

And then the real miracle took place. One of the students, with much emotion, said, "Brother Millet, we understand. We know what you feel."

I wept for a moment as I sat there and shared with them how much I loved them, how much I loved the Lord and his gospel, and how very much I wanted to share with them what I felt in my soul to be true and important. These feelings persisted throughout the day, and within a very short time there were no discipline problems to speak of. The Lord of love had moved in his mysterious way and had performed a great wonder. The miracle of love transformed me and a group of adolescents, teaching us a lasting lesson for life.

A more recent experience some years ago has also left its imprint on my soul. My wife received word from some of her high school friends that they would hold a class reunion in August. Not having seen many of her friends for years, Shauna was excited to be a part of it. She asked me if I would be willing to go with her, so I dutifully smiled and said it sounded like a lot of fun. (To be honest, I couldn't think of anything more deadly than spending five or six hours with a group of people I didn't know from Adam or Eve.) The plans went forward, and the long-anticipated day came. The evening was all I had anticipated it would be. My wife is a very loving person and has been forever, so she has a great many friends. She shook hands and hugged and greeted people with excitement for hours. Once in a while she would say to me, "Bob, could you wait here for just a second? I'll be right back. I want to go over and say something to Brenda (or Bill or Becky)." And so I stood there, not so patiently, wringing my hands, wondering why time seemed to stand still.

During one of those occasions, at about nine o'clock, I began to feel some bitterness toward my wife for leaving me alone. And then something happened. Something unexpected. I began to be taught and chastened through the medium of memory. I began to sense things I had never sensed before, such as how very much my wife had given of herself to stand by me for so long, to bear and basically rear our children, and to move forward through terribly challenging years without complaint. I reflected painfully upon how often I had been the center of attention, how often I had been the one to win the accolades, while she quietly and in the background went about the task of supporting and sustaining. I pondered in much anguish of soul on the times I had been insensitive or just plain uncaring. I don't think I am a mean or vicious person by nature, but I suddenly remembered the times through the years when I had failed to call home and indicate I would be late for dinner, all the times when in the name of physical exhaustion I had failed to assume my part of the parental obligation, and, most painful of all, the occasions when I knew she needed to be alone, to rest, to have time to herself, but when I had elected to do something other than be thoughtful. I didn't have much to say during the rest of the night, though I tried to act interested in what was going on.

Worrying that perhaps I was not having a glorious time, Shauna eventually suggested that we go home. I nodded. On the way home she turned to me and said sweetly, "I'm so grateful for my life." I was moved to tears but refrained from saying anything. Shauna has the ability to sit down and go to sleep in one motion, so we were home for only a very few minutes before she dropped off to sleep. After a restless night of facing up to who and what I had been, after sleepless hours with time spent on my knees begging for forgiveness and promising to be better, I awoke to a new view of things.

Let me say simply that without warning I was endowed with a depth of love and caring and affection that was beyond anything earthly. For days I was consumed with what I presume was charity, the pure love of Christ. I loved my wife, my children, and, above all, the Lord and his work with all my soul. For days I saw things as they really are. There is no way for me to describe the tenderness of feelings that accompanied what I can only label as a rebirth. I sang the hymns of Zion with a gusto and an emotion I had never known. The opening hymn in sacrament meeting that Sunday was "Because I Have Been Given Much." I went to pieces inside. The sacrament hymn was "I Stand All Amazed." I was unable to sing. The closing hymn was "How Great Thou Art." I could barely read the words of the hymn through my tears.

I read the scriptures with different eyes and attended to "new writing" everywhere. I prayed with real intent and with a sense of purpose that had seldom accompanied my petitions before. At the end of a glorious Sabbath day, as Shauna and I stood on our front porch on a breezy August evening, I turned to her and from the depths of my heart I said, "For reasons I do not understand, I have been given what I believe to be a foretaste of eternal life. If this is what it is like to dwell in the celestial kingdom with God, with my family, and among the Saints, then I will give everything, even my own life, to feel this forever."

Though I have not felt the same intensity of love since that time, except in flashes, the sobering and sacred memory and its effects linger. Nothing is quite the same to me now. I know, to some degree at least, what Nephi meant when he said he had been filled with God's love, even to the consuming of his flesh (2 Nephi 4:21). I know what Mormon meant when he spoke of the pure love of Christ, not alone as the motivation for acts of Christian service, but, more important, the means by which men and women are purified from sin and thereby become the sons and daughters of God (Moroni 7:48). The scriptures teach that we do not come to love as the Lord loves merely because we work hard at it. It is true that we must serve others, that we must concern ourselves with others' needs more than with our own. But that service and that outreach cannot have lasting effect, nor can it result in quiet peace and rest in the giver, unless and until it is motivated from on high.

We must ask for charity. We must plead for it. We must pray, as Mormon counseled, with all the energy of heart, that we might have it bestowed upon us (Moroni 7:48). As we do so, there will come moments of surpassing import, sublime moments that matter, moments in which we know that what we are feeling for God and his children is akin to what God feels for us. This dimension of love settles the hearts of individuals. It provides moral courage to those who must face difficult challenges. It unites and seals husbands, wives, and children and grants them a foretaste of heaven. It welds quorums and classes and wards and stakes into a union that is the foundation for Zion, the society of the pure in heart. And, once again, it comes from that Lord who is the Source of all that is godlike. It is thus to Jesus Christ that we look—in this endeavor, as in all others—to obtain charity, "the highest pinnacle the human soul can reach and the deepest expression of the human heart."[5] And, as the apostle Paul testified, there is a sacred sealing, a binding tie associated with that love. "I am persuaded," he wrote to the Romans, "that neither death, nor life, nor angels, nor principalities, nor powers, nor things present, nor things to come, nor height, nor depth, nor any other creature, shall be able to separate us from the love of God, which is in Christ Jesus our Lord" (Romans 8:38–39).

NOTES

1. Holland, *However Long and Hard the Road,* 107–9.
2. Ashton, Conference Report, April 1992, 25–26.
3. Yancey, *Jesus I Never Knew,* 147–48.
4. *Teachings of the Prophet Joseph Smith,* 240–41.
5. Hunter, Conference Report, April 1992, 85.

CHAPTER 18

LIVING IN THE WORLD

A ND SO WE ARE CALLED TO BE HOLY, to stand as lights in
a darkened world, to be different in order to make a
difference. And yet we live in the world. We do not
attend Church every day of the week, nor do many of us associate only with persons of our own faith or moral persuasion.
We have been called to come out of the world in the sense that
we are to forsake the ways and whims and voices and values of
the world and the worldly. In speaking of his chosen Twelve,
Jesus prayed: "I have given them thy word; and the world hath
hated them, because they are not of the world, even as I am not
of the world. I pray not that thou shouldest take them out of
the world, but that thou shouldest keep them from the evil"
(John 17:14–15).

There is a fine line here. While on the one hand, the Saints
of the Most High are to eschew all forms of evil and reject each
and every effort to dilute the divine, yet we are commissioned
to be a leavening influence among the people of the earth. We
cannot make our influence felt if we avoid the troublesome

issues in society and insulate ourselves and our families from today's challenges. For this reason, the leaders of the Church have chosen to speak out on certain matters. President Gordon B. Hinckley pointed out that "we deal only with those matters which are of a strictly moral nature or which directly affect the welfare of the Church. . . . We regard it as not only our right but our duty to oppose those forces which we feel undermine the moral fiber of society. Much of our effort, a very great deal of it, is in association with others whose interests are similar. We have worked with Jewish groups, Catholics, Muslims, Protestants, and those of no particular religious affiliation, in coalitions formed to advocate positions on vital moral issues."[1]

The way of the disciple is the way of holiness. It is a walk away from the ways of the world. It represents a genuine refinement of the soul, a cleansing of the inner self. Disciples who look ahead to that life which is in the Lord are far less prone to look back to the sinking standards of a sick society. Those who cherish virtue come to abhor vice. Those who are alive to the things of righteousness become dead to the ways of sin. And yet the Saints are invited to make their mark on society—to leaven the loaf. So it is that only as they first come out of the world, come to Christ, are lifted and built up and fortified in him, that they then seek to lift and build up and fortify others against the onslaught of avarice and the mountains of malevolence.

In a world in which values and direction are set by consensus, the Savior bids his disciples to cleanse the inner vessel, work in harmony with others of the household of faith, and seek to build up and establish the cause of Zion. Zion, the society of the pure in heart, a city of light, stands in marked contrast to Babylon, the abode of darkness, the gathering place of the worldly and the wayward. Babylon is the city of man; Zion is the city of God.

As members of The Church of Jesus Christ of Latter-day Saints, we have a responsibility to care for our neighbors and make a difference for good in their lives. Perhaps they will join the Church; perhaps they will not. But whether they do or not, we have been charged by our Lord and Master, as well as his chosen prophets, to love them, to serve them, and to treat them with the same respect and kindness that we would extend to a person of our own faith.

Unfortunately, religious discussions with those not of our faith too often devolve into debates or wars of words as a result of defensiveness over this or that theological issue. That need not happen. A few years ago, my colleague Brent Top and I traveled to another part of the country to meet with a well-known Evangelical theologian, author, pastor, teacher, and host of a radio broadcast heard throughout the nation. Brent and I had read several of this man's books and had enjoyed his preaching over the years. As part of an outreach effort to better understand those of other faiths (and to assist them to understand us a little better), we had visited such institutions as Notre Dame, Baylor, and Catholic University. It was in that context that we met the minister and attended his church both Sunday morning and Sunday evening, and in both meetings we were impressed with his expository preaching style.

The next day we met for lunch and had a wonderful, two-hour doctrinal discussion. I explained that we had no set agenda and were not exactly sure why we had chosen to visit him, except that we had admired his writings and wanted to meet him. We indicated that we had several questions we wanted to pose in order to better understand Evangelical theology. I mentioned that I oversaw the teaching of religion of almost thirty thousand young people at Brigham Young University and that I felt it would be wise for me to be able to articulate properly and accurately the beliefs of our brothers and sisters of other faiths. I hoped, as well, that they might make the effort to understand our beliefs so as not to misrepresent what we teach. The pastor was stunned that two LDS religion professors would visit him, but he was even more perplexed that we had read his books and enjoyed them! I took it a step further: I indicated to him that although there were some doctrinal chasms between us, I had quoted him in a few of my own books.

He said something like, "Look, anyone knows there are big differences between us, but I don't want to focus on those differences. Let's talk about Christ." We then discussed faith in Christ, justification by faith, baptism, sanctification, salvation, heaven, hell, agency and predestination, premortal existence, and a variety of other fascinating topics. We compared and contrasted, we asked questions, and we answered questions. In thinking back on what was one of the most productive and worthwhile learning experiences of our lives, the one thing that characterized our discussion—and the one thing that made the biggest difference—was the mood that existed there, a mood of openness, candor, and a general lack of defensiveness. We knew what we believed, and we were all committed to our own religious tradition. No one was trying to convert the other, but instead we were making an effort to understand one another. To be sure, we would have loved to have attended his baptism before we left, but that wasn't why we organized the visit, nor did we have any pretension to anything so bold. Likewise, the minister said to us, "Well, guys, obviously I would love to bring you around to my way of thinking, but it's nice to better understand you."

This experience says something about what can happen when men and women of good will come together in an attitude of openness and in a sincere effort to better understand and be understood. Some time ago my colleague Andrew Skinner and I visited Wheaton College, an outstanding Evangelical liberal arts school in Illinois. The purpose of our trip was simply to get to know some of the religion faculty there, to visit religion and history classes, and to become acquainted with the personnel and the resources at the Wade Center, which housed the largest collection of C. S. Lewis materials in the world. While there, we learned of an upcoming conference on Lewis and requested information. A call for papers was sent to me, and I made a proposal. The organizing committee accepted and explained that our perspective on Lewis would add a valuable dimension to the conference.

My paper provided an LDS perspective on the theology of C. S. Lewis, dealing mostly with why Lewis's thinking is so well received among Latter-day Saints. Professor Skinner and I had an unforgettable experience at that conference as well and came away richly blessed for the association, the conversations, and the exchange. Everyone there, faculty and students alike, knew of our religious differences, but no one seemed eager (at least in public) to label us as cultists or to suggest that we had some malicious purpose or ulterior motive for being there. The questions from students and faculty were courteous, thoughtful, and contributive to meaningful dialogue.

There is a very real sense in which the Latter-day Saints are a part of the larger "body of Christ," the Christian community, whether certain groups feel comfortable with acknowledging our Christianity or not. Given the challenges we face in our society—fatherless homes, child and spouse abuse, divorce, poverty, spreading crime and delinquency, spiritual wickedness in high places—it seems so foolish for men and women who claim to believe in the same Lord and Savior, whose hearts and lives have been surrendered to that Savior, to allow doctrinal differences to prevent them from working together. Okay, so this person believes in a triune God, that the Almighty is a spirit, and that he created all things *ex nihilo*. I believe that God is an exalted Man, that he is a separate and distinct personage from the Son and the Holy Ghost. She believes that the Sabbath should be observed on Saturday; her neighbor does not believe in blood transfusions. This one speaks in tongues, that one spends much of his time leading marches against social injustice, and a third believes that little children should be baptized. One good Baptist is a strict Calvinist; another tends to take freedom of the will seriously. And so on, and so on. Do we agree on the problems in our world? Do we agree on the fact that most all of these ills have moral or spiritual roots?

In the spirit of Christian brotherhood and sisterhood, is it not possible to lay aside theological differences long enough to address the staggering social issues in our troubled world? My recent interactions with men and women of various faiths have had a profound effect on me; they have broadened my horizons dramatically and reminded me—a sobering reminder we all need once in a while—that we are all sons and daughters of the same Eternal Father. We may never resolve our differences on the Godhead or the Trinity, on the spiritual or corporeal nature of Deity, or on the sufficiency of the Bible, but we can agree that salvation is in Christ; that the ultimate transformation of society will come only through the application of Christian solutions to pressing moral issues; and that the regeneration of individual hearts and souls is foundational to the restoration of virtue in our communities and nations.

One need not surrender cherished religious values or doctrines to be a better neighbor, a more caring citizen, a more involved municipal. Individuals can possess what my friend and colleague Richard Mouw calls "convicted civility"—they can be completely committed to their own faith and way of life but also be eager to learn and grow in understanding and thus to treat those with differing views with the dignity and respect they deserve as a son or daughter of God.[2] President Gordon B. Hinckley said of the Latter-day Saints: "We want to be good neighbors; we want to be good friends. We feel we can differ theologically with people without being disagreeable in any sense. We hope they feel the same way toward us. We have many friends and many associations with people who are not of our faith, with whom we deal constantly, and we have a wonderful relationship. It disturbs me when I hear about any antagonisms. . . . I don't think they are necessary. I hope that we can overcome them."[3]

I believe with all my heart in God and in his Son, Jesus Christ. I am committed to the doctrine and practices of The Church of Jesus Christ of Latter-day Saints; indeed, I have never been more committed to my own religious tradition than I am right now. At the same time, I have never been more liberal in my views—in the proper sense of that word *liberal*, meaning open, receptive—in regard to people of other faiths, especially Christian faiths. To some extent I am motivated in this direction by the following statement in the Book of Mormon: "For behold, the Spirit of Christ is given to every man, that he may know good from evil; wherefore, I show unto you the way to judge; for every thing which inviteth to do good, and to persuade to believe in Christ, is sent forth by the power and gift of Christ; wherefore ye may know with a perfect knowledge it is of God" (Moroni 7:16).

It is my conviction that God loves us, one and all, for I believe he is our Father in Heaven and that he has tender regard for us. I also feel strongly that, in spite of growing wickedness, men and women throughout the earth are being led to greater light and knowledge, to the gradual realization of their own fallen nature and thus of their need for spiritual transformation. C. S. Lewis once stated that there are people "who are slowly becoming Christians though they do not yet call themselves so. There are people who do not accept the full Christian doctrine about Christ but who are so strongly attracted by Him that they are His in a much deeper sense than they themselves understand." Lewis went on to speak of people "who are being led by God's secret influence to concentrate on those parts of their religion which are in agreement with Christianity, and who thus belong to Christ without knowing it."[4]

I am fully persuaded that we can be committed Latter-day Saints and that we need not compromise one whit of our doctrine or our way of life; indeed, our strength, our contribution to the religious world, lies in our distinctiveness. We are who we are, and we believe what we believe. At the same time, we can and should build bridges of friendship and understanding with individuals of other faiths. I believe this is what our Master would do, he who mingled with all elements of society and whose gaze penetrated the faces and the facades of this temporal world.

Once again, the people of the covenant have been charged to be "a chosen generation, a royal priesthood, an holy nation, a peculiar people; that [we] should shew forth the praises of him who hath called [us] out of darkness into his marvelous light" (1 Peter 2:9). Our religion is more than meat and drink, more than external trappings or successful activities. We strive to be more than clean-cut, well-dressed men and women, although our appearance should invite attention to rather than detract from our message. What we are, deep down to the core, is so much more important than what we are doing or what we may appear to be. Elder Bruce R. McConkie taught: "In the final analysis, the gospel of God is written, not in the dead letters of scriptural records, but in the lives of the Saints. It is not written with pen and ink on paper of man's making, but with acts and deeds in the book of life of each believing and obedient person. It is engraved in the flesh and bones and sinews of those who live a celestial law, which is the law of the gospel. It is there to be read by others, first, by those who, seeing the good works of the Saints, shall respond by glorifying our Father in heaven, and finally by the Great Judge to whom every man's life is an open book."[5]

NOTES

1. Hinckley, Conference Report, October 1999, 70.
2. Mouw, *Uncommon Decency.*
3. Cited in Dew, *Go Forward with Faith,* 576.
4. Lewis, *Mere Christianity,* 178.
5. McConkie, Conference Report, October 1968, 135.

STANDING IN HOLY PLACES

A FTER SPEAKING OF SOME OF the frightening events that lie ahead—for example, an "overflowing scourge" and a "desolating sickness" that will grip the land in the last days—the Lord added a prophetic insight that is simple and comforting: "But my disciples shall stand in holy places, and shall not be moved" (D&C 45:31–32). Likewise, after describing the wars to be poured out upon all nations, the divine directive comes: "Wherefore, stand ye in holy places, and be not moved, until the day of the Lord come" (D&C 87:8). There is safety in holiness, security in standing in holy places. The children sing it: "Keep the commandments; keep the commandments! / In this there is safety; in this there is peace."[1]

And what are the holy places in which we are to stand? They are the temples, the church houses, the homes of the Latter-day Saints. We are to become, first of all, a temple-centered people, a body of believers who are covenant conscious and focused on the things of eternity. Bearing in our souls "the testimony of the covenant" (D&C 109:38), we strive, as President Howard W. Hunter counseled us, to make the temple the great symbol of our Church membership.[2]

In that same spirit, we devote ourselves to faithful attendance and enthusiastic participation in the programs of the Church. This is the Lord's Church, and he is at the head of it. Through the principles, ordinances, teachings, and organized sacrifice provided by the Church, we purify our hearts, come to love and cherish one another, and mature in our relationship to God. We need the Church and feel undying gratitude for its restoration in these last days.

We go to church and to the temple to enter into sacred covenants, and we come home to keep those covenants and to live and practice the precepts we are taught there. The home is the most sacred of all institutions in the kingdom of God, for it houses the family—the most important unit in time and in eternity. We learn to be reverent and attentive to spiritual things in the temple and the church, but we apply these timeless lessons in the home. President David O. McKay thus taught that "a home in which unity, mutual helpfulness, and love abide is just a bit of heaven on earth."[3]

While the temple, the church house, and the home are and should be holy places, there is another holy place that in some ways is even more important to us. I speak of where we are, spiritually speaking, at any given time. For surely it is not where we are living or what edifice in which we are meeting that matters most; is it *how* we are living. And to the degree that we are living the gospel, doing our very best to keep our covenants, the Spirit of the Lord will be with us; where that Spirit is, there is peace and liberty and security. Therein is a holy place. "For I am able to make you holy," the Savior said, "and your sins are forgiven you" (D&C 60:7).

Our hope is in Christ. Our hope is not in mortal men and women, no matter how good or noble they may be. Hope is more than wishing, more than yearning for some eventuality or some possession. Gospel hope is a solid and sure conviction. Hope is expectation. Anticipation. Assurance. The Saints of the Most High—those who have come out of the world, put off the natural man, and put on Christ—these are they who are entitled to a "more excellent hope" (Ether 12:32). Hope flows from faith, faith in the Lord Jesus Christ. When we have faith in him, we believe in him—who he is and what he has done. Further, we believe he can do what he says he can do—make us clean and whole; make us pure before God the Father; make us happy, productive, and contributing members of his grand kingdom. Mormon taught: "And again, my beloved brethren [and sisters], I would speak unto you concerning hope. How is it that ye can attain unto faith, save ye shall [then] have hope? And what is it that ye shall hope for? Behold I say unto you that ye shall have hope through the atonement of Christ and the power of his resurrection, to be raised unto life eternal, and this because of your faith in him according to the promise" (Moroni 7:40–41; compare Ether 12:4).

And what is our indication that we are on course? How do we know we are growing in holiness? "Hereby know we that we dwell in him, and he in us, because he hath given us of his Spirit" (1 John 4:13). The presence of God's Spirit is the attestation, the divine assurance that we are headed in the right direction. It is God's seal, his anointing, his unction (1 John 2:20) to us that our lives are in order.

I can still recall very vividly the fear and awful anxiety that Shauna and I felt when we decided to purchase our first home. We had no money in savings, and though I held a steady job, it was one that did not bring a hefty income. Yet we knew we had to get started some time if we ever hoped to become home-owners. We determined to start slowly. A dear friend of ours, a fellow seminary teacher, located a place for us in his neighbor-hood. Another seminary teacher friend offered to lend us the down payment. It was at this time that Shauna and I became acquainted with the concept of "earnest money." We made a goodwill payment to the owner of the home, a small amount to be sure, but an amount that was sufficient to evidence our seriousness about purchasing the place. That amount was called the earnest money. It was a token payment, a gesture of our desire to acquire that home, a promissory note of sorts.

God works with us in similar ways. How can he commu-nicate to us that we are following a proper course? He can send his Spirit. The Holy Ghost thus represents God's "earnest money" on us, his down payment, his goodwill gesture and assurance to us that he is serious about saving us and that one day he will own us and claim us fully as his. "Now he which stablisheth us with you in Christ, and hath anointed us, is God; who hath also sealed us, and given the earnest of the Spirit in our hearts" (2 Corinthians 1:21–22). "Now he that hath wrought us for the selfsame thing is God, who also hath given us the earnest of the Spirit" (2 Corinthians 5:5). Finally, the apostle Paul wrote of the truth that the Saints had trusted in Christ "After that ye heard the word of truth, the gospel of your salvation: in whom also after that ye believed, ye were sealed with that holy Spirit of promise, which is the earnest of our inheritance until the redemption of the purchased possession, unto the praise of his glory" (Ephesians 1:13–14). In short, the same Spirit that eventually seals us up unto eternal life places a seal of approval upon our lives here and now. Though the fulness of the blessings of eternal life are not available until the world to come, the peace and rest and hope that are harbingers of those unspeakable blessings can and should be ours in this world.

We cannot overcome the world if we are worldly. We cannot overcome the world if our trust is in the arm of flesh (2 Nephi 4:34). And we cannot overcome the world if we live in a constant state of spiritual insecurity. Satan, the arch deceiver, is versatile and observant. As surely as the day follows the night, he will strike at our sense of security before God if we do not acquire that hope or assurance that comes by and through His Holy Spirit. We overcome the world through Christ—through being changed by Christ, captained by Christ, and consumed in Christ. At the Last Supper, Jesus declared to his disciples: "These things I have spoken unto you, that in me ye might have peace. In the world ye shall have tribulation: but be of good cheer; I have overcome the world" (John 16:33).

To what extent are we prepared to meet God? How ready are we to enter into heavenly places and to sit among glorified beings? Few of us would dare rush forward and volunteer to sign the list of names of the sanctified. But the revelations of God and the teachings of his servants affirm that if we are faithful in the Church, worthy of participation in the holy temple, and enjoying the fruits and benefits of the Holy Spirit—to that degree we are prepared to meet God.

We do not need to be possessed of an unholy or intemperate zeal in order to be saved; we need to be constant and dependable. God is the other party with us in the gospel covenant. He is the controlling partner. He lets us know, through the influence of the Holy Ghost, that the gospel covenant is still intact and the supernal promises are sure. The

Savior invites us to learn the timeless and comforting lesson that "he who doeth the works of righteousness shall receive his reward, even peace in this world, and eternal life in the world to come" (D&C 59:23). Peace. Hope. Assurance. These things come to us by virtue of the atoning blood of Jesus Christ and as a natural result of our wholehearted efforts to walk in holiness.

Our petitions rise up to him who has called us to holiness:

> *More holiness give me,*
> *More strivings within,*
> *More patience in suff'ring,*
> *More sorrow for sin,*
> *More faith in my Savior,*
> *More sense of his care,*
> *More joy in his service,*
> *More purpose in prayer.*
>
> *More gratitude give me,*
> *More trust in the Lord,*
> *More pride in his glory,*
> *More hope in his word,*
> *More tears for his sorrows,*
> *More pain at his grief,*
> *More meekness in trial,*
> *More praise for relief.*
>
> *More purity give me,*
> *More strength to o'er-come,*
> *More freedom from earth-stains,*
> *More longing for home.*
> *More fit for the kingdom,*
> *More used would I be,*
> *More blessed and holy—*
> *More, Savior, like thee.*[4]

I testify of the truths considered in this work. I know—

That a person may be fully active in the Church and yet feel an emptiness that bespeaks the need to grow and mature spiritually.

That each of us is in need of pardoning mercy and that our only hope for peace here and eternal reward hereafter is in and through the atoning blood of our Redeemer.

That the gospel of Jesus Christ is a positive and progressive movement onward and upward, and that the Spirit of the Lord, if we give heed to its influence, will prompt and motivate us to climb higher.

That as a peculiar, or purchased, people we have been called to come out of the world, to forsake Babylon, and to enter the realm of divine experience.

That spiritual growth is to take place every day of our lives, and that we should be striving to keep every day holy.

That we are called upon to eschew the world and embrace the gospel now, to improve and forsake today, not tomorrow.

That some things simply matter more than others, and that certain commitments of time and resources here will reap grand dividends hereafter.

That as we deny ourselves of ungodliness and bridle our appetites and passions—that is, as we gain the victory over self—we acquire that quiet confidence and assurance that testify of heaven's approbation.

That the Saints of the Most High can and should enjoy sweet communion with the God of us all through meaningful prayer.

That the challenges and vicissitudes we experience here are intended to refine and educate us, if we choose to trust in the Lord and his purposes.

That the Saints are encouraged to balance their zeal with knowledge and wisdom, to stay in the mainstream of the Church, and to proceed along the strait and narrow path in a quiet and consistent manner.

That in the midst of the babble of voices and the noise of a fallen world, we can and should seek out opportunities to ponder and reflect upon things of eternal worth.

That while our growth in spirituality takes place line upon line, we must continue to learn and stretch and expand our knowledge and broaden our spiritual experience.

That as we climb the mountain of spirituality we are awed and staggered by the majesty and power and goodness of God and the beauties of his creations.

That how we view the Lord affects how we live the gospel: if in every move we are fearful that God may smite us should we fail or fall short, our labors will not be fruitful.

That if we are to ascend to those heights where Gods and angels dwell, we must be willing to submit, surrender, and walk the path of the lowly Nazarene.

That in the long run we assess our level of holiness by the manner in which we manifest the fruit of the Spirit and thus love and serve the children of God.

That while we are not of the world, in order to make a difference in the world for good, we must live in the world.

I know, further, that there is a God; he is our Father in Heaven. I know that Jesus of Nazareth is the Christ, the Promised Messiah, the Hope of the Ages, and that salvation comes in and through his atonement and in no other way. I know that there is a plan and purpose to life, a plan of salvation, the great plan of the Eternal God, and that that plan, revealed in the earliest ages of earth's history, has been restored to the earth through the instrumentality of a modern prophet, Joseph Smith. I know, as I know that I live, that Joseph Smith was called by God to stand as the head of this final dispensation as a legal administrator (one through whom priesthoods and powers were restored) and a revealer of divine truth (one through whom doctrine and precepts, once lost to the world, have been restored). In addition, my witness is current: I know that the keys of the kingdom of God have been committed to man on earth, that apostles and prophets walk the earth and direct the destiny of the Lord's kingdom, and that The Church of Jesus Christ of Latter-day Saints is the custodian of the fulness of the everlasting gospel. These things I have come to know, with certainty, by the power of the Holy Ghost.

Finally, I know that the purpose of this life is to prepare to meet God. God is at work in our lives; he and we are involved in a team effort to save our souls. Like Paul, I am confident "that he which hath begun a good work in you will perform it until the day of Jesus Christ" (Philippians 1:6). Over time and through experience, we learn to trust in and rely upon the merits, mercy, and grace of the Holy Messiah and do all we can to be cleansed of carnality and equipped and empowered with righteousness. As we do so, we come to see things as the Gods see them, things as they really are. We see things like Christ does because we have become like Christ. The apostle John wrote: "Beloved, now are we the sons [and daughters] of God, and it doth not yet appear what we shall be: but we know that, when he [the Savior] shall appear, we shall be like him; for we shall see him as he is. And every man that hath this hope in him purifieth himself, even as he is pure" (1 John 3:2–3). Some three centuries later and a continent away, the Nephite prophet Mormon added the significant detail that it is through the receipt of that highest and holiest of spiritual endowments—charity, the pure love of Christ—that the true followers of Jesus Christ are known, "that when he shall appear we shall be like him, for we shall see him as he is" (Moroni 7:48). The psalmist thus declared, "As for me, I will behold thy face in righteousness: I shall be satisfied, when I awake, with thy likeness" (Psalm 17:15). God grant that it may be so with each of us.

NOTES
1. *Hymns,* no. 303.
2. Hunter, Conference Report, October 1994, 8.
3. McKay, *Gospel Ideals,* 477–78.
4. *Hymns,* no. 131.

SOURCES

Andrus, Hyrum L., and Helen Mae Andrus, comp. *They Knew the Prophet.* Salt Lake City: Deseret Book, 2000.

Ballard, M. Russell. "Building Bridges of Understanding." Address at institute of religion, Logan, Utah, 17 February 1998. Typescript.

Ballard, Melvin J. *Melvin J. Ballard—Crusader for Righteousness.* Salt Lake City: Bookcraft, 1966.

Benson, Ezra Taft. "A Message to the Rising Generation." *Ensign,* November 1977.

———. *Teachings of Ezra Taft Benson.* Salt Lake City: Bookcraft, 1988.

Bonhoeffer, Dietrich. *The Cost of Discipleship.* New York: Macmillan, 1976.

Clark, James R., comp. *Messages of the First Presidency.* 6 vols. Salt Lake City: Bookcraft, 1965–75.

Clarke, Adam. *Adam Clarke's Commentary on the Bible.* Abridged by Ralph Earle. Grand Rapids, Mich.: Baker Book House, 1967.

Conference Report of The Church of Jesus Christ of Latter-day Saints. April 1899 through April 2000.

Dew, Sheri L. *Go Forward with Faith: The Biography of Gordon B. Hinckley.* Salt Lake City: Deseret Book, 1996.

Evans, Tony. "The Priority of Worship." Transcript of radio address, Dallas, Texas, n.d.

Faust, James E. *Finding Light in a Dark World.* Salt Lake City: Deseret Book, 1995.

Fitzmyer, Joseph A. *The Gospel According to Luke, X-XXIV.* Anchor Bible series. New York: Doubleday, 1985.

Frankl, Viktor. *Man's Search for Meaning.* New York: Washington Square Press, 1985.

George, Bob. *Classic Christianity.* Eugene, Oreg.: Harvest House Publishers, 1989.

Hafen, Bruce C., and Marie K. Hafen. *The Belonging Heart.* Salt Lake City: Deseret Book, 1994.

Hinckley, Gordon B. *Teachings of Gordon B. Hinckley.* Salt Lake City: Deseret Book, 1997.

Holland, Jeffrey R. *Christ and the New Covenant.* Salt Lake City: Deseret Book, 1997.

———. *However Long and Hard the Road.* Salt Lake City: Deseret Book, 1985.

Holy Bible. Authorized King James Version. Salt Lake City: The Church of Jesus Christ of Latter-day Saints, 1979.

Hunter, Howard W. Conference Report, April 1992.

Hybels, Bill, and Rob Wilkins. *Descending into Greatness.* Grand Rapids, Mich.: Zondervan, 1993.

Hymns of The Church of Jesus Christ of Latter-day Saints. Salt Lake City: The Church of Jesus Christ of Latter-day Saints, 1985.

Journal of Discourses. 26 vols. Liverpool: F. D. Richards & Sons, 1851–86.

Kimball, Spencer W. *Faith Precedes the Miracle.* Salt Lake City: Deseret Book, 1974.

———. *The Miracle of Forgiveness.* Salt Lake City: Bookcraft, 1969.

Lee, Harold B. *Stand Ye in Holy Places.* Salt Lake City: Deseret Book, 1974.

———. *Teachings of Harold B. Lee.* Selected by Clyde G. Williams. Salt Lake City: Bookcraft, 1996.

———. "To the Defenders of the Faith." *Improvement Era,* June 1970.

Lewis, C. S. *Letters to Malcolm: Chiefly on Prayer.* San Diego: Harcourt Brace & Co., 1964.

———. *Mere Christianity.* New York: Touchstone Books, 1996.

———. *The Great Divorce.* New York: Touchstone Books, 1996.

———. *The Problem of Pain.* New York: Touchstone Books, 1996.

———. *Letters of C. S. Lewis,* rev. ed. San Diego: Harcourt Brace & Co., 1993.

Lyman, Francis M. "Proprieties in Prayer." *Improvement Era,* April 1947.

Lyon, Jack M., Jay A. Parry, and Linda R. Gundry, *Best Loved Poems of the LDS People.* Salt Lake City: Deseret Book, 1996.

McConkie, Bruce R. *Doctrinal New Testament Commentary.* 3 vols. Salt Lake City: Bookcraft, 1965–73.

———. *Doctrines of the Restoration.* Edited by Mark L. McConkie. Salt Lake City: Bookcraft, 1989.

———. *Mormon Doctrine,* 2d ed. Salt Lake City: Bookcraft, 1966.

———. *The Mortal Messiah: From Bethlehem to Calvary.* 4 vols. Salt Lake City: Deseret Book, 1979–81.

———. *The Promised Messiah.* Salt Lake City: Deseret Book, 1978.

———. "The Seven Deadly Heresies." In *Brigham Young University Speeches of the Year,* Provo, 1 June 1980.

McEntyre, Marilyn Chandler. "Silence Is to Dwell In." *Christianity Today,* 7 August 2000.

McKay, David O. *Gospel Ideals.* Salt Lake City: Improvement Era, 1953.

———. *Man May Know for Himself.* Salt Lake City: Deseret Book, 1967.

————. *True to the Faith.* Comp. Llewelyn R. McKay. Salt Lake City: Bookcraft, 1967.

Mouw, Richard J. *Uncommon Decency: Christian Civility in an Uncivil World.* Downers Grove, Ill.: Intervarsity Press, 1992.

Nibley, Hugh. "Clementine Recognitions," III, 34; cited in *Since Cumorah.* Salt Lake City: Deseret Book, 1988.

Oaks, Dallin H. "Family History: 'In Wisdom and Order.'" *Ensign,* June 1989.

————. "Our Strengths Can Become Our Downfall." *Brigham Young University 1991–92 Devotional and Fireside Speeches.* Provo, Utah: University Publications, 1992.

————. "Sin and Suffering." In *Brigham Young University 1989–90 Devotional and Fireside Speeches.* Provo, Utah: University Publications, 1990.

Pace, Glenn L. *Spiritual Plateaus.* Salt Lake City: Deseret Book, 1991.

Packer, Boyd K. *Let Not Your Heart Be Troubled.* Salt Lake City: Bookcraft, 1991.

————. "Self-Reliance." Brigham Young University Speeches of the Year, Provo, 2 March 1975.

————. *That All May Be Edified.* Salt Lake City: Bookcraft, 1982.

————. "The Fountain of Life." Brigham Young University fireside address, 29 March 1992.

Parry, Catherine Corman. "'Simon, I Have Somewhat to Say unto Thee': Judgment and Condemnation in the Parables of Jesus." In *Brigham Young University 1990–91 Devotional and Fireside Speeches.* Provo, Utah: University Publications, 1991.

Paulsen, David L. "Early Christian Belief in a Corporeal Deity: Origin and Augustine as Reluctant Witnesses." *Harvard Theological Review* 83, no. 2 (1990).

————. "The Doctrine of Divine Embodiment: Restoration, Judaeo-Christian, and Philosophical Perspectives." *Brigham Young University Studies* 35, no. 4, 1996.

Prayer. Salt Lake City: Deseret Book, 1978.

Random House College Dictionary, rev. ed. New York: Random House, 1988.

Rasmussen, Dennis. *The Lord's Question.* Provo, Utah: Keter Foundation, 1985.

Roberts, B. H. *Seventy's Course in Theology.* 5 vols. Salt Lake City: Deseret News, 1857–1933.

Romney, Marion G. "Caring for the Poor and Needy." *Ensign,* January 1973.

Smith, George Albert. *Sharing the Gospel with Others.* Selected by Preston Nibley. Salt Lake City: Deseret Book, 1948.

Smith, Joseph. *Lectures on Faith.* Salt Lake City: Deseret Book, 1985.

————. *Teachings of the Prophet Joseph Smith.* Selected by Joseph Fielding Smith. Salt Lake City: Deseret Book, 1976.

Smith, Joseph F. *Gospel Doctrine.* Salt Lake City: Deseret Book, 1971.

Smith, Joseph Fielding. *Doctrines of Salvation.* 3 vols. Compiled by Bruce R. McConkie. Salt Lake City: Bookcraft, 1954–56.

Stanley, Charles. *The Blessings of Brokenness*. Grand Rapids, Mich.: Zondervan, 1997.

Stott, John. *Life in Christ*. Wheaton, Ill.: Tyndale House Publishers, 1991.

Taylor, John. *The Mediation and Atonement*. Salt Lake City: Deseret News, 1970.

Top, Brent, and Bruce Chadwick. *Rearing Righteous Teens in Today's Wicked World*. Salt Lake City: Bookcraft, 1998.

Webster, Noah. *American Dictionary of the English Language*. 1828. Reprint, San Francisco: Foundation for American Christian Education, 1980.

Yancey, Philip. *The Jesus I Never Knew*. Grand Rapids, Mich.: Zondervan, 1995.

INDEX

from God, 207, 211–12. *See also*
Love
Conception: into a world of sin,
11–12; as the vehicle for
transmitting the effects of the Fall,
13
Condescension of Christ: necessity
of, 183–84; Joseph Smith on,
184–85; purposes of, 184–85; as
a pattern for mankind, 185–86,
194
Confidence, *vs.* fear, 179
Conscience, 179–80
Consecration: devoting ourselves to
the gospel cause, 190; giving up
earthly properties, 190–93; Bruce
R. McConkie on living the law of,
191–92; Dietrich Bonhoeffer on
earthly possessions, 192
Conversion: as a process, 3–4; *vs.*
having a testimony, 3–4;
definition of, 4
Cooperation, and discipleship, 189
Covenant: gospel of Jesus Christ as a,
180–81; God as the controlling
partner in the gospel, 227–28
Discipleship: as a downward path,
183, 185–86; condescension of
Christ as a pattern for, 185–86,
194; winning in modern society,
186; losing ourselves in the Lord,
186–89; putting off the natural
man, 187–88; Ezra Taft Benson
on putting God first, 188; having
an eye single to God's glory, 188;
cooperation and, 189; Howard W.
Hunter on meekness in, 189–90;
consecration as a necessary
element of, 190–93; Bruce R.
McConkie on consecration,
191–92; Joseph Smith on
sacrifice, 193; humility and,
193–94; forsaking worldly ways,
214–15
Discouragement, dealing with:

discouragement as tool of Satan,
112; accepting life's difficulties
and challenges, 112–15; Boyd K.
Packer on life's struggles, 113; C.
S. Lewis on questioning the
necessity of suffering, 114;
learning from sin, 115–16;
choosing our response to trials,
116–19; Viktor Frankl on
choosing our attitude, 117;
having a willingness to be
"broken," 117–18; experience
with wayward loved ones,
118–19; turning to the Lord for
hope and healing, 118–20;
Howard W. Hunter on Christ's
healing hands, 119; seeking help
from others, 119; acknowledging
our accomplishments, 120;
Harold B. Lee on the healing of
sick souls, 120; Lorenzo Snow on
focusing on others' needs,
120–21; losing ourselves in
service to others, 120–21; looking
toward the day when all wrongs
will be righted, 121–22; Boyd K.
Packer on enduring unsolvable
problems, 122; Bruce and Marie
Hafen on forgiving, 122–23; Ezra
Taft Benson on righteously
hanging on, 123
Doctrine. *See* Gospel teaching and
learning
Earnest money: experience buying
first home, 225–26; Holy Ghost
as God's, 226
Emptiness, feelings of, 1–4
Ends *vs.* means, significant life events
as, 4–5
Eternity to eternity, Joseph Fielding
Smith on, 163
Excess, avoiding: staying in the
mainstream of the Church, 125;
going beyond the expected,
125–26; Dallin H. Oaks on failing

to consider individual
circumstances, 126; riding gospel
hobbies, 126–29; Joseph F. Smith
on treating a fragment as the
whole, 127; Joseph F. Smith on
gospel hobbies, 127–28; Harold
B. Lee on pride produced by
gospel hobbies, 128; Bruce R.
McConkie on gospel hobbies,
128–29; experience with man
desiring perfection by age thirty,
129–30; forcing spiritual things,
129–31; Boyd K. Packer on
forcing the Spirit to respond, 130;
experience with woman seeking
to make calling and election sure
by age fifty, 130; building
reservoirs of spiritual experience
gradually, 130–31; Spencer W.
Kimball on accumulating spiritual
preparedness, 130–31; perfection
as a process, 131; living by every
word of God, 131–32; adding to
or taking away from doctrine,
132; looking beyond the mark,
132–34; Dean L. Larsen on going
beyond the mark of wisdom and
prudence, 133–34; becoming
spiritually mature, 134

Faith: Joseph Smith on, 85; prayer
of, 85–87; C. S. Lewis on actions
vs., 181

Fall of Adam: effect on man's
relationship with God, 11; Joseph
Smith on, 11; and man's
propensity to sin, 11–13; spiritual
death the result of, 15. See also
Atonement of Christ

Fanaticism, gospel. See Excess,
avoiding

Fasting: purposes of, 87–89; David
O. McKay on, 89

Faust, James E., on Sabbath
observance, 60

Fear: standing before God with fear
and trembling, 158; as a motive
for faithfulness, 172–73, 175–77;
parable of the talents and,
173–76; vs. reverence, 175; in the
unproductive steward's
perspective on the master,
175–76; vs. confidence, 179; vs.
heeding our conscience, 179–80;
dispelled by understanding the
grace of Christ, 180–81; Joseph
Fielding Smith on looking back,
182

Feelings, Charles W. Penrose poem
on schooling our, 94–95

First Vision: Gordon B. Hinckley on,
161; understanding the doctrinal
profundity of, 161–62

Forgiving, Bruce and Marie Hafen
on, 122–23

Frankl, Viktor, 117

Fruits of the Spirit, 202–3

Fundamentals, focusing on, 76–77

"Getting real," 46–47

Gifts of the Spirit: as a sign of the
true Church, 201; as a way for the
Lord to bless people of the
covenant, 201–2; vs. fruits of the
Spirit, 202–3

God the Father: characteristics and
attributes of, 162–63; as our God
throughout the eternities,
163–64; reverencing vs. fearing,
175; actions affected by our
perspective on, 175–77; as the
controlling partner in the gospel
covenant, 227–28

Gospel hobbies. See Hobbies, gospel

Gospel teaching and learning: adding
to or taking away from doctrine,
132; experience of wife in
maternity ward, 143–44; Boyd K.
Packer on teaching truths at the
wrong time, 144; observing
gospel prerequisites, 144–48;
Joseph Smith on starting right,

145; experience with missionary companion, 145–47; following the lead of the General Authorities, 148–49; staying open to new truths and new insights, 149, 220–21; importance of both testimony and knowledge, 149–51; Joseph F. Smith on gospel knowledge, 150; B. H. Roberts on gospel knowledge, 150–51; focusing on doctrine, 151–52; Boyd K. Packer on studying doctrine, 152; Bruce R. McConkie on teachers' and students' responsibilities, 152–53; responsibility of teachers, 152–53; repetition in, 153–54; digging deeper, 154–55; institutional *vs.* individual responsibility for, 154–55; parable of the hidden treasure, 155. *See also* Excess, avoiding

Grace of Christ: remembering the price of Christ's grace, 45; gospel of Jesus Christ as a covenant, 180–81; understanding of, as an antidote to anxiety, 180–81; C. S. Lewis on actions *vs.* faith, 181. *See also* Atonement of Christ

Granger, Oliver, 176

Hafen, Bruce and Marie, on forgiving, 122–23

Hamlet, 104

Happiness: experience with young couple searching for, 1–4; Joseph Smith on, 5

Hinckley, Gordon B.: on moving forward without hesitation, 35; on joining mainstream America, 37; on Sabbath observance, 59–60; on the First Vision, 161; on the Church speaking out on legislation, 215; on relationships with those of other faiths, 220

Hobbies, gospel: riding gospel

hobbies, 126–29; Joseph F. Smith on, 127–28; Harold B. Lee on pride produced by, 128; Bruce R. McConkie on, 128–29

Holland, Jeffrey R.: on the pure love of Christ, 178–79; on love in marriage, 199–200

Hollywood, as the source of standards, 38

Holy, definitions of, 37–38, 45–46

Holy Ghost: as the agent of the new birth, 16–17; as a sanctifier, 44; allowing the Spirit to be in control, 64–65; Boyd K. Packer on forcing the Spirit to respond, 130; fruits of the Spirit, 202–3; presence of, as assurance our life is in order, 225–27; as God's "earnest money" on his children, 226

Holy places: standing in, 223; temples as, 223–24; church houses as, 224; David O. McKay on homes, 224; homes as, 224; Howard W. Hunter on temples, 224; where Church members are spiritually as, 224

Home, David O. McKay on, 224

Hope: turning to the Lord for, 118–20; in Christ, 225; assurances of, through the Holy Ghost, 227

Humility, and discipleship, 193–94

Hunter, Howard W.: on prayer, 101; on Christ's healing hands, 119; on meekness, 189–90; on temples, 224

Immorality, destruction of love by, 196–97

Insensitivity: sensitivity to others as a sign of spiritual maturity, 204, 206; experience with inquisitive ward member, 205; experience of father returning to Church activity, 205–6

Tolerance, as an excuse for condoning sin, 39–40

Tongue, controlling our: experience with insensitive comment to mother, 93–94; Charles W. Penrose poem on schooling our feelings, 94–95; Boyd K. Packer on spiteful remarks, 96

Top, Brent, 41, 106, 216

Trials. *See* Discouragement, dealing with

Trusting in the Lord, 63–64

Webster, Francis, 118

Wells, John, 141–42

Wheaton College, 218

Winning, in modern society, 186

Wordsworth, William, 38

World, living in the: and forsaking worldly ways, 214–15; and being a leavening influence, 214–16; Gordon B. Hinckley on the Church speaking out on legislation, 215; joining with those of other faiths to establish the cause of Zion, 215–16, 218–20; experience discussing doctrine with Evangelical pastor, 216–18; experience visiting Wheaton College, 218; Gordon B. Hinckley on relationships with those of other faiths, 220; acting with "convicted civility," 220–21; C. S. Lewis on those who belong to Christ without knowing it, 221; becoming a holy people, 222; Bruce R. McConkie on living the gospel, 222

Worldliness, turning away from: Gordon B. Hinckley on joining mainstream America, 37; striving to become holy, 37–38; looking to Hollywood for standards, 38;

our day as the day of Satan's power, 38; William Wordsworth on, 38; experience with weary BYU student, 39; condoning sin in the name of tolerance, 39–40; Dallin H. Oaks on allowing strengths to become weaknesses, 39–40; judging righteous judgment, 39–40; keeping our thoughts pure, 40–41; Brent Top on grasping the iron rod, 41; Dallin H. Oaks on avoiding pornography, 41; living on the edge, 41–42; filling our life with light and truth, 42; George Albert Smith on staying on the Lord's side of the line, 42–43; drawing lines of demarcation, 43; distancing ourselves from the world, 44; enjoying the Holy Ghost's sanctifying influence, 44; remembering the price of Christ's grace, 44–45; honoring our covenants, 45; rejecting Satan's lies about sin, 45; becoming perfect in Christ, 45–46; experience with alcoholic friend, 46–47; "getting real," 46–47; putting away the things of this world, 47

Worship: definition of, 158; Bruce R. McConkie on forms of, 158–59; patterning our lives after Christ as, 159–61; through the singing of hymns, 170; expressions of gratitude as, 170–71

Young, Brigham: on the influences of the flesh and the spirit, 10; on living beneath our spiritual privileges, 15; on nourishing the spirit, 53